A

DAMAGED

WOMAN

THE SEQUEL

SUNNI T. CONNOR

DISCLAIMER

This book and any intent included in this book is not to be an act of intent or any way permitted as legal use for revenge or legal action towards the author. Although names and dates have been changed to protect the original characters, no characters are a certain individual or any certain story to depict that individual or character. The author or publishing company is not responsible for any belief of a character or event. While this book is based on the author's life events, names and identifying details have been changed to protect the privacy of the possible similarity of the people involved.

This book may not be reproduced in whole or part, in any form or by any means, electronic or mechanical, including photocopying, recording or by any information storage and retrieval system now know or hereafter invented, without written permission from the author

ISBN-978-0-578-70047-2

I dedicate this book to my loving parents, my beautiful children and to the families who lost.

Table of Contents

Chapters

INTRODUCTION *Letter*

Dear Reader,

Wow! Did you come back for more? So, you made it through a DAMAGED little girl. Did you need therapy? Did reading my life story make you want to hurt someone? Did it make you feel grateful for your childhood? Could you relate to the pain I endured? If you didn't read DAMAGED little girl, READ IT! I'm not big on introductions. What is there really to introduce in life? Why sell yourself or anything to convince someone to be curious enough to know more? I could give you a fantastic introduction, but I prefer you to dig deep and get straight to the story. I prefer you to open your mind and close your assumptions. Even if you read DAMAGED little girl, you still have no idea where this reading journey is about to take you. Instead of a formal introduction, I'll use this time to recap the first book.

Desmond and Queen are my parents. They were in love. They dated, they had massive sex and "POOF," I arrived. They thought I'd be a boy, but nope I came out fully loaded with a vagina. I was in love with my mother, almost obsessed. She was indeed the Queen of my life. I loved my father just as much. I was my father's twin and a true Daddy's Girl. My parents and I went through many traumatic events, but we overcame them with God, time, and faith. My father's mother died of cancer, and I lost my grandmother at the age of two. She loved me dearly; it was a significant loss for our family.

I moved in with my mother's godmother, where a perverted sick freak molested me. I called him, "The Devil." That Bitch thought it was ok to put his bone in my 4- year- old mouth. I moved to Perkins projects, where I fought, loved, and got thrown out after a traumatizing police encounter. From there, I moved in with my lovely Aunt Shelby. While living with my Aunt Shelby, I was enrolled in a school where I had to fight five ugly beasts because they were unattractive and unhappy from what they saw in the mirror.

I moved on to meet my "Neighborhood Brothers." I had a close friendship with Morris. Sadly, Morris was murdered after winning a fistfight. I met the love of my life named Chico. He was gorgeous and everything I yearned for in a boy. Chico and I lost contact after the crooked cops raided our house, which is how I moved in with my father. During the time I lived with my father, I lost my uncle to suicide, kidnapped my cousin, and went to live with my godsister, Honey. While spending time with Honey, I lost my virginity to a Hennessey smelling, little dick, Black Puerto Rican! Sadly, he couldn't fuck worth a damn—what a waste of a tight vagina. I later went on to sleep with a guy who actually could fuck. I sold him some pussy, and he blessed me with my first trip to the OBGYN to get some antibiotics after burning me with his dirty penis. Sex was more of a burden than it was pleasurable.

I worked at a few jobs with the Hispanics to make my way. I was underage, and the jobs allowed me to save money to move out on my own, which I desperately wanted. I was the first minor ever to finish high school at night in Baltimore city. I completed my entire senior year at night school, which was a massive accomplishment since life seemed to be haunting me.

I met Row. Oh, how I loved Row. He pleased me with my first sexual orgasm, my first emotional attachment to a man besides my father, and he financially spoiled me. He also left me. He left me broke and damaged, almost unfixable. When an item comes DAMAGED, do you try to fix it, or do you send it back for a new item? Throughout life, I got shipped back with a "DAMAGED LABEL." Now I am a woman, and I'm still damaged, but I'm not broken. So, get the tools out and fix me, this package is now undeliverable.

Yours truly,

A Damaged Woman

CHAPTER *1*

THE AFTERMATH

In life, one must walk a long path of darkness to see a small fracture of light. After Row's death, I was in a very dark place. I continued to wake up in the hope of finding some light. I searched for the strength to keep living. The impact a human can have on another person's life when you allow their energy to come into your heart can be overwhelming. Well, I had no choice but to get through it. The day I looked in the mirror at an unrecognizable reflection is the day I realized I had changed for the worse. I had lost so much weight. I could see the veins coming out of my neck; it was alarming. I was frail and weak. I looked terrible, and I felt awful.

The sudden change in my reality was crucial to why my life went towards darkness. Row left me with some shit to handle. I rarely paid attention to the amount of money I spent living on a Hustler's salary. I was spoiled, and I needed to fill the void. I had an addiction. I was addicted to drug money. I was too immature to comprehend the consequences of fast money. I had extensive spending habits and a lifestyle to uphold. I would soon have to come off that high horse or go to the lowest of the low to stay on it.

One would assume the bullshit in my life would've stopped after Row's death. Sadly, for me, the shit got worse. My life slowly started deteriorating. All I had left of Row were memories, I kept every word and every conversation Row, and I ever shared dear to my heart. I called those conversations, "Preparing Sunni for life." One of the biggest lessons I learned from Row was the ability to respect money. He told me to pay myself first, no matter the amount of money I earned. I took that as, *eat the bread but save the crumbs.* He was trying to teach me to spend the bills but save the change. We had many of these talks, and I always remembered those little cliché lessons. Thankfully, I listened carefully to the, *save your money lesson.* I had $9,000 at the time of his death. That was nothing compared to what I could've saved, but it was something. I was lucky to have any money, considering how reckless I spent the fast money.

Time heals once again. About nine months after Row's death, I got better. I gained my appetite back and started pulling myself together. I told myself, *fuck love*. I shut down from who I was. All I knew was I never wanted to feel that strongly for another person again. I didn't want to be vulnerable. I didn't want to take a chance of possibly getting hurt. I tried to avoid another deep grieving spell. I related *love to pain*.

I woke up one morning, ready to live again. I was disgusted with my appearance and even more disgusted with my lack of energy to fight for life. My grief turned into anger. I thought, *who the fuck is Row to leave me broken, depressed, frail, and weak?* I blamed Row for his death. It was the only way I could get through it. In my mind, he left me. *How sick of me to think this way?* I wiped my salty tears off my cheeks. I was young, and I had my whole life ahead of me, so it was about time I started to live it.

I still worked at the same company in Hunt Valley, and I still lived in the same apartment on Mt. Royal Terrorist. I came home from work one day, and I saw a van with tinted windows. I noticed it, but I thought nothing of it. I continued to walk into the apartment building, but I felt as if someone was watching me. I could feel their glare keen on my neck. I looked around my surroundings; there was no one in sight. I put my key in the front door, opened the door, and dropped my shoes by the entrance before walking towards the kitchen. I opened the refrigerator to get some water; then I heard a faint sound. I softly closed the fridge and slid open the kitchen cabinet drawer to grab a knife. Just as I grabbed the knife, I heard my upstairs neighbor.

"Sunni!" he yelled. He startled me, and I dropped the knife. I slowly walked to my back door without opening it.

"How long were you here?" I asked in a confused tone. My heart still raced as if I was in danger.

"Only ten minutes, I was waiting for you," he responded.

"Waiting for me at my back door in the dark? Why didn't you just call my cell?" I asked as I unlocked the door and let him in the kitchen.

"It's okay, Sunni. I didn't mind waiting. I need to know you are safe," Victor said as he turned on my kitchen light as if he was in his apartment.

My neighbor's name was Victor. His face annoyed me. He was light-skinned with freckles, his hair was dirty brown, and he wore shoes that came off the JC Penny rack. They were Nike's, but who would ever know what kind. After Row died, Victor would come to check on me and bring me food, straighten up my apartment or bring over a DVD to watch. At first, he consoled me, and I honestly thought he was my friend. I figured he pitied me, and he felt it was his obligation to feed me since I didn't care enough to feed myself. Every day after work, he would bring me a chicken box with the chicken fried hard with a half and half lemonade iced tea. Just one time, I mentioned the chicken was good, and he assumed I wouldn't mind eating it every day. I told him he didn't have to bring me food, but he had to be sure he would see me. He had to see me.

Victor started expressing his love for me. I bluntly told him I was still in love with Row, and I wasn't interested in dating. I explained how I thought we should stay friends. I looked in his eyes whenever I talked to him because he would often shy away. Why would a man shy away from direct eye contact from a woman? This was a question I asked myself many times. *Does he look away because I'm so damn thin? Maybe he looks away because my personality is aggressive? Perhaps he was on, "America's Most Wanted," and he didn't want me to recognize him.* In my mind, the possibilities were endless. Instead of keep wondering about his lack of eye contact, I decided to ask him.

"Why don't you look me in my eyes?" I asked.

"I don't look at you because I'm in love with you, and I'm afraid of how I will react if you don't love me back," Victor responded.

His response blew my fucking mind. *Wait! He was scared of how he would react? That statement scared the fuck out of me.* I was naïve enough to ignore it. He was a clown, and I was from the streets. In my mind, I would blow his fucking head off if he tried me. Row left me with a sweet 9-millimeter gun ready for use with one bullet in the chamber. Now I talk that talk, but I didn't want to actually kill someone, especially not my friend Victor.

Meet Victor, he's my freckled face, Psycho maniac, stalker, friend, and neighbor. What's the fucking odds that I would get stuck with a "Lifetime Movie" neighbor? I took Victor's aggressive pop-ups too lightly. Well, here's when things took a turn for the worse. I started going back out with my friends. I gained a few of my pounds back, I went shopping, and I came and left as I pleased. The historic building, I lived in was once so beautiful to me. It looked like a castle inside; it had sculptures of huge lions throughout the building. The swivel steps leading to the 2nd-floor apartments were elegant and ancient. The building features that I once loved so dearly became frightful, only because a particular person in the building became frightful.

I was out hanging with my friend Tesa who I knew from Curley Street. I was intoxicated, and in no way should I've been driving under those conditions. I was drunk and sloppy. After I dropped Tesa off, I sat in my car and cried. Slobber, snot, and grief filled my face. That's what drunk people do. They either talk too much, they want to fight, they're overly friendly, or they cry. This night, I was the cry baby drunk. I managed to drive myself home with only knocking off my side mirror. I parked the car out back and stumbled to my back door. It was dark and quiet. I felt like someone was out there with me.

I rushed back to my car and drove to the front of the building so I could see the streetlights. I put my key in the tall, heavy building doors. The doors were so heavy, and when they shut, there was an echo in the building. Soon as the door shut, I jumped. All the building lights were off. I immediately took off my high heeled shoes so I could walk comfortably to my door. I put my hands out so I could feel around to avoid bumping into something. I got to my front door, and I stepped on something soft.

"Fuck, what the hell was that?" I cursed in a whispered voice. I looked down, and I saw one single white rose taped to a card. I picked it up with hesitation, quickly glanced around, and proceeded to put my key in the door. I hurried into my apartment and closed my front door. I sat on my cream leather sofa and opened the anonymous card which read,

"Hi, my love. I saw this rose and thought of you. I'm sorry I had to throw your chicken away because you were out too late. I look forward to seeing you tomorrow."

I thought, *oh, hell no!* This mother fucker is crazy. What the fuck is up with him and all this damn chicken? All I been through, I be damn if I will let some pussy ass man scare me. All the signs were there. I ignored them. I thought Victor was just lonely, and it was okay to be his friend. I never lead him on, kissed him, or even touched him. He wasn't my type; actually, no man was my type at the time, my type was dead.

I was grieving when Victor conveniently started coming around. Victor was always just there. He was there to help me with my groceries. He happened to be there to hold the door open for me at night. He would be at my door with a flashlight when the building's power would go out from a storm. I always said, "Thank you," and smiled before going back to whatever I was doing. I remembered our first conversation; it became important when things got crazy. I sat on the back-deck area, polishing my toenails, listening to sad music.

"Hello. Sunni, right?" Victor asked in a friendly tone.

"Hi. Yup, my name is Sunni. How did you know?" I questioned, never looking up from the nail polish.

"I'm guilty. I peeped on your mailbox," Victor admitted with his hands up in the air.

"Oh. And what is your name?" I asked unfazed.

"My name is Victor. I live on the second floor," he stated as he pointed up the steps.

"Nice to meet you, Victor. Well, let me get out of your way so you can make your way upstairs," I said, finally looking up at Victor.

"You are not in my way. It's funny we are just formally meeting. I always help you around the building, and we never actually held a conversation."

"I know funny, right? Thanks for always helping me. Sorry if I've been rude. I'm just going through some stuff."

"Did you and your boyfriend break up? I notice he's not around anymore," Victor said too eagerly before he could catch his tone.

"You notice a lot, I see. No, we didn't break up. He's deceased."

"Oh, I'm so sorry. Please forgive me for intruding. I'm going to get a chicken box from the spot on North Avenue. Do you want one?"

"No, thanks."

"Come on now; you have to eat. Everything will be okay," Victor insisted, and I agreed to accept the chicken box.

That was the beginning of Victor and the chicken chronicles. First, it was him bringing me chicken all the time. Then it was little gifts with notes such as candles, flowers, and small teddy bears. The notes were friendly. They were mainly sympathy, or *"I'm praying for you,"* notes. Nothing to be alarmed about, well so I thought. That all changed on this one Saturday morning.

I had been out until 3:00 in the morning. It was a hot summer night. I smoked so much weed around the way that I'd forgotten my own name. I was stoned. I sat at a STOP sign for at least 3 minutes, waiting for the light to change. Yeah, I was high, alright. I finally made it home after driving only about 5 miles per hour. All I wanted to do was shower and crash in my king-sized bed—what a simple request for such a complicated life.

I walked into the apartment building, and I felt relieved the lights were on. I started to think someone was purposely turning the lights off. Sometimes they were on and sometimes they weren't. There was a card at my front door that I decided to leave there. I didn't have time for Victor's stupidity or his stupid little gifts. I had a mission, wash my ass, cum, and go to sleep. I walked in my front door, and the apartment was freezing. I didn't remember cutting the air down so low. I assumed I did it by mistake. I walked to the thermostat, and I was surprised to see it was set at the lowest temperature. I felt it was odd.

I grabbed Row's towel and put one of his wife-beater shirts on the bed. I usually slept naked, but I wanted to snuggle in his shirt since the apartment was so cold. I had on a peach-colored loose-fitting dress with some Bebe sandals. Just a simple outfit I had thrown on earlier that day. I removed the dress and put the sandals in my closet. I sat on the bed, unsnapped my bra, and looked around the room. It seemed cleaner than I remember leaving it. I was so high off the weed; I couldn't remember if I had cleaned up or not.

I looked at my body in the full-length mirror in my bedroom, and I admired myself. I smiled at the fact I gained my little ten pounds back. My neck was full, and I was back my original weight of 125 pounds. I looked at my extremely flat stomach and my perky breast. I turned to the side to check out my curvy ass, which was always a little something to grab on, considering I was slim. I appreciated being slender with a round booty versus a flat butt. I softly rubbed my nipples and watched myself in the mirror. My breasts were sensitive, and every soft touch sent a message to my girl that we needed to release. My own touch excited me, which was confirmed by my juices that slowly ran down my leg. I walked towards my shower ass naked with Row towel laid across my shoulder. I ran the hot water only; I slid the glass shower door open and stepped in the shower.

I patiently waited for the steam to cover the glass door before I laid my head back and allowed the water to forcefully hit my face. I closed my eyes and reminisced on the many showers Row and I had together. I imagined his hand touching the back of my neck and slowly working towards my breast. I grabbed the removable shower head that was well worth the investment after Row died. A great showerhead became my side piece. I enjoyed the sensation of the pulsating water touching my skin. I moved the showerhead around my clitoris in a circular motion. The feeling was too intense, so I adjusted the settings to a softer function. As "my girl" (my vagina) and I started to enjoy our shower, I heard a loud sound come from the kitchen. I thought, *fuck! I'm almost there. I should just finish releasing before someone come and kill me.* So, I continued pleasing myself. My body tensed up as I enjoyed releasing my juices. I was instantly disgusted as I often was after masturbating. I missed Row dearly, and I had no interest in another man touching me, just yet. So, this was the aftermath, I'm young, hot, and I'm dating a showerhead.

I turned off the water so I could hear the intruder who invited themselves to my house. I couldn't see out of the glass shower door; it was fogged up from the steam. I prayed when I slid the door open; there wouldn't be anyone waiting with a gun in my face. I got out of the shower and put my towel around my wet naked body. I stood there for a minute to try to warm my skin. The apartment was still freezing. I thought, *what if someone really is out there?* I had no choice but to see. I opened the bathroom door, and I felt uneasy. I shut the door back and decided to come up with a plan before I left the bathroom. I tried to calculate how fast I could run to my room and grab the gun. I was too high to focus. Paranoia took over my body.

"Do you need help, my Love?" Victor asked as he continued to step over all the parts to the new lock.

I ignored him and rolled my eyes. I continued to read the directions as he sat there for a few minutes, staring at me. I refused to acknowledge him. *The nerve of that sick freak to offer to help. The nerve of him to act like it's normal to have keys to my house.* Now Victor is everywhere. He's around my car, my front door, my back door, the supermarket. Wherever I am, there is Victor.

Me threatening him or cursing him out did not affect him. I believe it turned him on more. My voice excited him. My anger towards Victor gave him more pleasure in some sick way. He felt it was his obligation to make me feel better, instead of leaving me alone when I got upset. He bought me flowers and apologized. I never took his gifts. I grew deep hate for him. He even washed my car twice a week without my permission, and he left a stupid love note on the windshield every time. He made my life miserable. Many nights I would stay at my friend's houses to avoid running into Victor.

I went to an open house on Liberty Avenue. It was a two-bedroom house apartment. The apartment I initially saw was gorgeous and had everything I wanted in an apartment. The landlord asked me a series of questions.

"Do you have any children?" she asked.

"No, just me," I replied.

"I may rent this apartment to another young lady with a son since it's a two-bedroom, and you don't have any children," she implied.

I was instantly disappointed, and she saw it in my face. I left and went back to Stalkersville, where Victor was torturing me. I cried from anger. The thought of spending another waking moment in that apartment building with my stalker was overwhelming. I wanted that apartment, and I declared it mines. My aggressive desires lead me to the power of God and the energy of the universe. I first used this power when I was 17 years old. I wanted to finish high school at night, and the counselor told me it couldn't be done. I believed that it could be done, and I spoke it into existence. I didn't know how to use the power of God and belief, but I was manifesting my desires without knowing it. The next morning the landlord called.

"Sunni? I'm sorry. I rented the apartment you viewed to another tenant," she said soon as I answered the phone.

"Okay. Thanks for letting me know," I responded in a calm but disappointed tone.

"No problem. I liked you so much that I still wanted to help you. Do you have time to look at the basement apartment in that same house? It's smaller, but it's nice."

"Sure. I can come right over," I responded with excitement.

When I arrived to see the apartment, it was perfect. It had everything I needed. The walls were made of brick, and they were unfiltered, untouched, and attractive. The rawness of the walls attracted me to the apartment. The master bedroom was huge and could easily fit my king-sized bed. They only flaw was the low ceilings. I had gotten spoiled with the high ceilings at Mt Royal Terrorist. I didn't manifest the first apartment, but I got something better. I should've paid attention to my ability to make things happen in my favor.

The next afternoon, I went to three supermarkets to ask for their old boxes so I could start packing. I wanted to move out within two days. I also wanted to move out in the middle of the night to avoid Victor following me to my new house. I tried to walk through the back door in the hopes of not running into Victor. Well, I wasn't that lucky. He happened to be right by my door, waiting to take what he thought was owed to him. He stood there with his legs crossed, leaning against my back door in a linty black shirt with loose-fitting shorts, black socks, and a pair of jail slippers.

"Hey, Sunni! I have a surprise for you in the house!" he said as he slowly slid my door open.

"How did you get back into my house? I'm sick of playing these games with you, Victor. I have told you many times I am not interested. Now you leave me no choice," I yelled. I proceeded to walk away from my apartment.

"Sunni, I know you think Row don't want you to move on, but I assure you, he wants you to be happy. I will make you happy," he said. He reached his arm out to invite me to join him at my house.

"Don't you ever say Row name again. It's not about him. You are sick, and I don't want you. You need help, Victor." I turned my back to walk towards my car. I felt a strong arm grabbing me and pulling me towards my apartment.

"What did you call me?" Victor asked, grabbing my arm with much force.

"Get the fuck off of me!" I screamed. Victor said nothing but continued to pull me. I lost my balance, and I fell hard on the concrete. "So, you going to drag me?" I asked while screaming.

He looked away and continued to drag me. I thought, *I have to get back on my feet, focus Sunni.* I let him continue to pull me while I focused on standing up. I put one foot on the ground, grabbed his arm for a grip to lift my other foot, and placed it on the ground. Now I was standing again. No way will I let this clown ass bitch rape me.

Although I was back on my feet, he still had the power; he was a man with a lion's strength. I was a woman with the strength of a baby monkey. The math wasn't adding up. We were getting close to the door, and a panic feeling took over my body. I knew if he got me in the apartment, it would go bad either way. Option one, I would get raped, and that would destroy me as a woman. Option two, I may get raped, but I may get to my gun, which always had one bullet in the chamber, and I'd blow his fucking head off. Both options would surely destroy my life. So, I decided not to make it inside the apartment at all. He had physical strength, but I was mentally more robust.

"Victor, wait, slow down. Look, I've been through a lot, and sometimes I can't see what's right in front of me. Calm down. This is not the way we want this to happen," I proclaimed.

"Sunni, I don't want to fight with you. I've been patient. I want to be with you, and rejection hurts. Give me a chance to make this right," he pleaded.

As he was pouring out his heart, I kicked him right in his man piece. Now he was physically weak. I kicked him in his dick again. He screamed and reached out to punch me. I moved back and started hitting him with all my might. Yes, I could've escaped. I could've screamed louder for the neighbors to hear me. I could've got to safety, but this fight was well overdue. I wanted to fight—what better time than when he was weak. So, I put in work. I punched, scratched, kicked, and even bit him. He defended himself, but I felt nothing. Finally, a neighbor came and started cursing at him while calling the police. I ran to my car and pulled off with speed.

I called my mother and told her what happened. She came back to the apartment with me to help me pack. I moved out the next morning, fearless. The funny thing is, in the hood, we live by a street code so much that I never called the police on Victor. I never filed a report, a restraining order, or anything. We don't call the police no matter what's happening, even if a stalker is torturing you. I didn't tell my father or anyone in my family what was happening. I don't know why I kept it to myself. I only told my mother. I had men in my family who could've handled the situation right away. I think deep inside; I still looked at Victor like a friend. That was the sweetness in me that life couldn't take from me. I still have my sweetness. I'm more like the sour patch candy; first, I'm sweet than I'm bitter. Don't corner a sweet person as strength comes with a sour punch!

CHAPTER 2

MY GHOST BITCH

One door closes, and another door opens. I was almost 19 years old, and I was living in my 3rd apartment. I went from renting a room to moving into one luxury apartment after another. I didn't slow down long enough to realize how strong I was or to compare my accomplishments to other 18-year-old adults that still lived at home. I was a survivor. Shit happened, I got weak, I fixed it, I got stronger, and then moved on. This pattern became the unfortunate cycle of my damaged life. I couldn't understand how to change this period of my life, so it became my new normal.

A few months went by, and I stopped thinking about Victor. I erased him altogether. Once I got away from him, he no longer existed. I started decorating my new apartment. It was vital that I made it feel like home. My new apartment was God's plan. God strategically placed me there so I could mentally get stronger. God always has a plan. I'm not sure why I had to be scared half to death by a stalker for me to move out, but it worked. My new apartment lacked memories of Row. He didn't exist in my new world, not his smell, not his clothes, no laughter, no sex, no remembrance of Row at all. The new environment had officially closed my mourning chapter. It was time for me to move on; it was time to live again. Not that I wouldn't have any more bad days, but with no constant reminder of Row in my new house, my days got a lot easier.

Let me introduce you to My Ghost Bitch, also known as Sugar. She's one of a kind. I call her My Ghost Bitch because she always disappears, yet she always around right when I need her. When her presence is not required, the Bitch goes ghost. Her energy is like the mist of a ghost; she just shows up without warning and disappears without warning. Although she fades out, her spirit is always around even when she's not. Let's go back to the past for a minute so I can explain how I met Sugar. I met her in the 10th grade. I sat at a filthy desk at a High school I attended in East Baltimore. The nasty desk had gum stuck underneath the storage holder, profanity written in permanent marker all over the top, and a sticky substance inside the body of the desk. I was sitting alone daydreaming about how I would love to be anywhere but at that horrific school.

Sugar walked in the classroom with some freshly done braids, all name brand clothes, and a confused look. She was small but not skinny, thick in the right places but not fat, caramel but not light-skinned. I looked up at her and turned away. Far as I was concerned, she was just another chick walking into a classroom full of unmotivated teens and a very annoying soft-spoken teacher who was clearly out of her league working in such a hard-core urban school. She sat down, and I continued my daydream. I admired my ability to go to the world of daydreaming where I could get lost, escape my present, hide from my circumstances, and be whomever I so desperately wanted to be.

The moment she became more than just a girl walking into a classroom, is when she raised her hand and requested to go to the office for her new schedule. The teacher, Mrs. Bask, asked could someone walk her. I volunteered. I would do anything to get out of that disappointment of a classroom. I walked her to the office, and we talked the entire time. Lake Clifton was a big school, the hallways were long and wide, so any walk was a long walk. That day, we became friends. I didn't know it at the time, neither did she.

I discovered she was my friend when I was absent from school one day just a few weeks later. A girl named Nika, who I fought years ago down Perkins projects, was talking trash about fighting me again. Fighting and drama was the miserable mindset of most Baltimore girls. We fought in the 2nd grade, and now we were in high school, and the poor girl was still angry? What a waste of years spent being bitter. Nika openly talked trash about me to the classroom. Sugar confronted her.

"Why are you talking about someone who is not here?" Sugar asked.

"Why do you care?" Nika responded with an attitude.

"I just think it's cowardly to talk about someone who's not here to defend themselves," Sugar said nonchalantly.

"Since you care so much, can you defend yourself? Do you want to take her place and get your ass whipped?" Nika asked.

Before Sugar could say another word, she turned to the side, when she turned back towards Nika, she was caught with a surprise punch to the jaw and that fast they were fighting. When I returned to school, I was informed about the fight and instantly grew a deep respect for My Ghost Bitch for standing up for me. Her courage to defend my name immediately created a friendship. Nika was not a little petite girl. She was tall and thick. She was not the size you would prefer to fight if you had a choice. So that's that. Now you know how I met Sugar. Now you will understand how she slithered in my life, and soon, you will know how deep our connection goes.

I was in my new apartment with an oversized white crop shirt, some leggings, and a pair of fluffy socks. It was my clean up outfit. I had the music blasting, and I was dancing and dusting. I heard the phone ringing over the music. I turned down the radio station 92Q and answered the phone with deep heavy breaths.

"Hello," I said out of breath as I ran to the phone and picked it up right before the last ring.

"Hey, Boo. What are you doing?" My ghost Bitch asked.

"Oh, hey, Sugar. Nothing much, cleaning and dancing," I responded.

"I was thinking about you. I'm glad you are finally away from that psychopath! Girl, I have to tell you about Bear," she exclaimed.

"What Bear do now? Y'all crazy! Did he buy you a car yet?"

"Nope, not yet. Girl, we are thinking about having a threesome. He wants to introduce another female into our sex life. To be honest, I'm curious too," she admitted.

"Bitch, you crazy as shit!" I screamed with excitement. "Since when are you curious about females? You sure it's not more of his idea?" I asked.

"Yes, I'm sure smart ass. We mutually want to experiment in our sex life. I mean our sex good now, but we are young, and it sure would be lovely to have an extra person to do extra shit."

"Yeah, sometimes I do be wishing there were an extra tongue or set of hands to help complete the job. Well, let me know how that goes. I can't wait to hear that juicy story. You not worried about the other female trying to take your man?"

"No! Bear knows I will kill him. He knows not to play with me. We discussed a clean stranger with no strings attached or someone that we trust. We both got tested for STDs and stuff; that way, we can feel safe. That's enough about me. Are we still going out next weekend? Don't be bluffing," Sugar asked.

"Yup, we are still going. I'm a hit the Gallery up Friday to grab a fresh outfit. Girl, let me finish cleaning just in case I pick up some dick sometime soon cause this masturbating shit is getting old."

"Girl, your ass is still crazy. See you this weekend Boo," she ended the call with laughter.

I hung up the phone and continued to clean my apartment. The weekend came fast, and it was time to party. I purchased myself a fresh outfit from the Gallery. It was a tight jean skirt with a transparent yellow crop shirt. I did my hair in a flexi rod set. My hair was dyed blonde on the tips, and it was shiny and bouncy. I was excited to see My Ghost Bitch. I hadn't seen her since Row funeral. During the time I was grieving, she showed up for support. She always showed up when I needed her.

Bear was Sugar's boyfriend. He was short but not shorter than us but just not tall. He had a lovely caramel complexion with cornrows. Bear dropped Sugar off at my apartment, and I drove us to a club in downtown Baltimore. I met a guy who was continuously buying me drinks. I was too young to purchase alcoholic drinks. Sugar didn't drink alcohol. She was on the other side of the club talking with some people we knew from high school. The guy grabbed my waist, and I swayed my hips from side to side as we danced. He breathed heavily on my neck. I took my arms and put them behind his neck, and I embraced his body closer to mines as I rocked my hips from side to side.

"Damn, you smell good," he whispered in my ear with hot liquor breath.

"Thanks," I smiled and continued to dance.

I looked around the crowd to find Sugar. I didn't see her right away. I turned to the side, and there she was glaring out the side of her eyes as I danced. She was so overprotective. I smiled at her. She was always on point, and I should've known her eyes weren't too far off me. She watched me like a settled owl. The guy was growing a hard erection as the dance got more intense. I pulled his head closer to my neck.

"You want my girl, don't you?" I asked in a low, seductive voice.

"Who? Your girl over there? Nah, I want you, Shorty," he awkwardly stated.

"No, I'm talking about this girl," I responded as I pointed to my vagina.

"Hell Yeah, I want that girl. Do you want my boy?" he asked as he grabbed his hard-stiff penis.

"What, boy? I have yet to feel a boy. All this dancing and I haven't met your boy yet!" I sarcastically joked.

He grabbed my hand with force and placed it on his penis. I snatched my hand away. I was the one in control, and I wanted him to know that. I put my hand back on his penis and squeezed with force as I slowly went down his jeans until I reached the head of his penis, which was almost by his knee. I thought, *oh, this baby is thick, he had more boy than I was ready for. Was that a penis I just touched or a baby horse? What the fuck?* His enormous sized penis made me nervous. I turned to look at the guy in his face.

"Oh, I see your father blessed you," I said with a smirk.

"Yeah, he did. You trying to meet my boy or what?" he asked with a cocky look on his face.

"No, thanks. I would like to keep my vagina walls. My girl is young tight and petite. She would prefer to avoid a horse dick from fucking her shape up," I said with a grin.

"Yo, you are hilarious. Never quite heard it that way before. So, no play, huh?" he asked.

"Nope, but thanks for the drinks and the dance," I replied. I shook my head at his surprisingly big penis and walked towards Sugar.

Sugar saw me walking towards her and gave me the, *"are you ready to go?"* look. I motioned my head to let her know I was ready to go. We got in the car and discussed the big penis guy that I danced with throughout the night. We laughed so hard at how fast I ran from the long snake that sat in between his legs. I was a big flirt, and even if he had a regular-sized penis, I wasn't giving up any random club coochie. We stopped the car at a red light, and at that moment, I looked up at Sugar and fell into deep thought. I wondered, *why is she still in my life? We have nothing in common, she doesn't drink, she doesn't smoke, she partied a little, but she was always completely sober, we don't share the same interests or hobbies. But she's my friend, and I love her.* We had absolutely nothing in common, yet I was still drawn to her. We were connected, and no one understood our friendship. Not even me sometimes.

I wasn't prepared for what waited for me at my apartment. It was "the plan." Apparently, I was part of this plan, and I would soon find out. I ran down the apartment steps with speed to use the bathroom.

I opened the front door and left my keys dangling in the keyhole. I dropped my purse in the middle of the floor and ran to the back of the apartment bathroom.

"Hey, Boo! Bear is going to pick me up. Is it cool if he comes in for a minute?" Sugar yelled as she took the keys out of the door and picked my purse up off the floor.

"Of course, Girl. Oh my God, I had to pee so bad," I yelled from the bathroom.

It felt like I peed a stream of water going down a tall mountain. I released my urine, and it felt so good. I took a baby wipe that I kept in a basket near the toilet and wiped my girl before I flushed the toilet. I washed my hands and fixed my hair in the mirror. I opened the bathroom door and was face to face with Sugar.

"My bad, I had to go too. Bear is out there," Sugar stated.

"It's cool, those public bathrooms be disgusting. I was holding it forever, and that liquor is not my bladder's friend," I said as I walked towards the dining room.

"Hey, Pretty girl, how you been? I like your new spot," Bear said as he looked around to compliment what I had done with my new place.

"Hey, Bear. Thanks. I've been chilling. What about you?" I asked.

"Better now. So how did you feel when Sugar told you about our proposal?" Bear asked.

"What proposal?" I ignorantly asked. Sugar walked into the room while shaking the excess water off her hands.

"Oh, I didn't get a chance to talk to Sunni about that yet," she said in an annoyed tone towards Bear.

"Talk to me about what? Y'all know I'm a little slow when I'm drunk," I joked.

"Well, Bear and I want you to be the one we have our threesome with," Sugar confessed in a low tone.

"What, Bitch? Maybe I didn't hear you clearly," I yelled out of surprise.

"You heard her right," Bear interrupted.

"Bear is attracted to you, and I trust you. I feel you would be the perfect person to experience our threesome. Are you down?" Sugar asked boldly.

I got quiet, really quiet. I had never been with a girl, nor did I want to risk destroying our friendship. I never looked at Bear in that kind of way. My friend's men were off-limits. My mind was racing with excitement and fear. I could easily say no, and we could laugh and move on from the topic, but I was curious. I had no desire to eat pussy, but I thought it would be a thrill to be with two people at once.

"Ok, I'm down," I nervously answered.

"That's what the fuck I'm talking about," Bear blurted out with excitement.

"Just one thing, though; I'm not interested in sucking on a vagina, but I'm down for anything else," I said.

"That's cool, Sunni. Having a threesome is our fantasy for our personal experience. No pressure on you at all. Bear go massage Sunni's legs like you do mines," Sugar demanded, ultimately taking control of the threesome.

Bear walked over to me and got on his knees. He took both of his hands up and down my legs, squeezing my thighs in and out. I was nervous. His hands were warm but felt rough like a man's hands would feel. Sugar stood up behind my chair and softly played in my hair, stroking it towards the back. She slowly and patiently moved all of my hair out of my face. Bear continued to massage my legs. Sugar's hands were soft and delicate as a rose. She started massaging my neck, and my body got hot. Sugar moved her hands from my neck down to my breast. She lightly twirled my nipple in a circular motion. She then took off my shirt and unsnapped my bra. My breasts fell comfortably in their position.

"Bear, suck her breasts," Sugar said softly.

Bear came in between my legs while still being on his knees and begin to suck my breasts softly. He put his hand up my jean skirt and started playing with my girl. I never wore panties, so he had easy access to my overly excited wet vagina. The touch of my juices excited him as he sucked my breasts more intensely. Sugar came from behind me and softly licked my nipples. I looked down at both of them and couldn't believe what was happening.

"Let's go to the room," I lightly whispered.

They both stood up and started tongue kissing and rubbing on each other's bodies. Bear removed Sugar's shirt, and her breast sat plump and firm in her bra. I sat in the same position, watching them interact with each other. Bear kissed her as he unstrapped her bra. Her breast fell out of the bra, and Bear started squeezing them while moaning. I admired her beautiful full breasts, they looked similar to mines, but hers were fuller. They continued to kiss, and then Sugar reached her hand out for me to join them. I looked at her perfectly manicured hand and paused because her hand was the reminder that I was having this interaction with Sugar. Bear reached his hand out as well, and I stood up to lead them to my bedroom.

We entered my dark bedroom, and I removed the rest of my clothes as they undressed each other. We all stood ass naked, kissing and touching each other. I looked down at Bear nice sized man piece, which wasn't too big nor too small. I smiled at him. I looked at Sugar perfectly trimmed vagina, and I was so happy I had shaved my girl earlier that day. The embarrassment I would've felt if I had a bush in between my legs would've been a disgrace. Thankfully, I didn't make that mistake.

I laid on the bed first to give the signal we could get comfortable. Soon as I put my head on the pillow Bear was in between my legs sucking on my clitoris and Sugar was under Bear sucking his man piece. I played with my nipples as I closed my eyes to enjoy the sensations. I decided to open my eyes to watch Sugar. I got more and more excited watching Sugar please Bear. He moaned and licked my girl more intensely. My mind was exploding, and I couldn't believe the fun we were having. I moaned as Bear almost sucked me into an orgasm. Before I allowed myself to climax, I pulled his head up, and I moved his penis out of Sugar's mouth, and I begin to please him, and he moaned while grabbing my head as Sugar sucked and licked his balls. Bear's eyes rolled in the back of his head, and he was in pure ecstasy. We both felt his body getting weak, and we both slowed down to avoid a premature nut.

"Bear, don't cum yet. You better hold that shit back," Sugar demanded.

"Yeah, you better," I agreed.

"Oh, I'm good. Don't worry about me. I'm trying to enjoy this night," Bear insisted.

Sugar stopped sucking Bear's balls and started pleasing my girl. Her tongue was soft, and her mouth was hot. She licked my clitoris softly, and then she would softly suck. Her rhythm and pattern made me have a fast orgasm. She knew exactly what a woman liked, and she treated my girl just as she would have treated her own. I moaned louder as I reached an ultimate climax. I continued to please Bear as I could taste the pre-cum leaking from his hot penis.

Sugar released Bear's penis by gently pulling it past my perfectly shaped plump lips. She jammed his fully erected penis in my vagina. The feeling was unbearable. He stroked slow, and with hip motion as I laid on my back, Sugar laid beside me, sucking my breasts. I pulled her towards me so she would be close enough for Bear to taste her girl as he penetrated me. She pushed his head deep in her pussy as he fucked me harder.

"Remember, don't cum in her," Sugar whispered.

"I know baby, switch positions," he said.

Bear penetrated Sugar from the back, they stood up, and Sugar arched her back. Her moans turned me on. I laid under Sugar and sucked her breast the way I liked mines sucked. He fucked her harder and rougher, and she moaned louder and louder. She grabbed my head more rooted in her breasts, and I sucked them a little harder. She screamed as she was having an orgasm. I pumped my vagina against her vagina and reached my full climax, and our juices ran together as we laid in exhaustion. Bear got the hint and released as well. His sperm aggressively squirted out all over Sugar's ass.

We all fell on the bed. We were silent. The only sound in the darkroom was heavy breathing. Bear laid in the middle with his arms around both of us. For the moment, we all just remained quiet and enjoyed what just happened. Our bodies were hot and sweaty. I had one hand on Bear's hard masculine chest as my other hand comfortably fell around Sugar's waist. Finally, I broke the ice.

"This was an adventure, but we could never do this again," I said.

"Never! It was a one-time thing," Sugar agreed.

"It was definitely worth the experience though," Bear added with a smirk.

"Yes, it was," Sugar agreed. "Bear you are to never contact Sunni, as we agreed," she firmly told Bear.

"Yeah, I know. I would never disrespect you, Wifey. Never!" Bear assured as he kissed Sugar's lips.

"I would never disrespect you either. You have been my A1 since day one. We had fun, and that's it. It will never leave this room," I added.

"I love y'all," Sugar said to both of us.

We laid there for a few more minutes, and then they got up to get dressed. I threw on a robe and walked them to the front door. We said our goodnights and I went to bed alone. I was fully relaxed. We never spoke about this day again. It was like it never happened. Until NOW! I've exposed our dirty little secret. This secret was to rest at our graves, but I'm not dead, nor are they. Sugar will likely read this chapter and get ghost. She'll disappear like the foggy mist in the deep dark sky. Sugar may be upset with me, but she'll return. Our friendship is strong and unbreakable, which is why she's My Ghost Bitch.

CHAPTER 3

MY HEART CAN BEAT

A heart is the most crucial organ in our bodies. It's a mystery how it dedicates so much work, effort, and commitment to keep us alive. A heart can also feel emotions and pain. It's an organ that functions directly with the brain to allow feelings and emotions. It's not just a machine, it's the heart baby, and I found my perfect heartbeat. I'll introduce you to him in just a bit. First, we must talk about the creator.

Around the way, I hung in this house down the hill called "The Flat." I first went to The Flat with my old neighbor Tesa. I knew Tesa from Curly Street, and we sometimes hung out. Tesa was a Bitch most of the time, but she had a kind heart and a giving spirit. She was dark, slim, a little tall with attractive features. She had dark black eyebrows, a cute little nose, and milky dark skin. She was pretty, but her attitude at times sucked. I was closer with our other mutual friend, Missy who lived down the hill. Missy had a caramel complexion, long eyelashes, a long-shaped head like mines, and she was attractive as well.

The Flat was a jump off house. We had so much fun doing nothing. We smoked weed, got drunk, cracked on each other, listened to music, and sometimes cooked Sunday dinner for all the round the way guys. We were in the company of murders, robbers, and drug dealers, the slimiest and greatest of East Baltimore. It was the problem house on the block. It was the house the neighbors despised. They secretly wished the house would burn down, and then they would never have to see anyone of us again. For me, the house was somewhere to chill before we went to the club or just to hang out on a rainy day. I wasn't a regular at The Flat, but I was there enough. I always worked so I could never hang out as much as Tesa and Missy, but it was a guaranteed adventure when I did come out.

On this day, I met the creator of my heartbeat. His name was Marco. He was tall with broad shoulders, he had a caramel complexion, with a killer smile. Marco was handsome and immediately caught my eyes. Marco wasn't dressed like the typical street guy, he wore work clothes, and he moved differently. I, too, had on work clothes; I had on a black and white blouse, black slacks, and some red heels that were killing my feet. He noticed me as well; we both had that working look.

I was at The Flat sitting outside on the roof of my car talking shit. I had a 1991 white Oldsmobile Cutlass Supreme that I bought for $1500 after I crashed the car Row helped me buy before he died. Missy needed a blunt and Tesa, and I wanted a drink. I jumped off the hood of my car and popped my trunk open to find some flip flops or something to relieve my feet from the high heeled shoes. Missy and I walked to the liquor store, she went inside to get a blunt, but they wouldn't serve us alcohol because she lost her ID and I wasn't old enough to buy it. I was only 18, almost 19 years old. Usually, someone outside the bar would buy it for us, but no one was there, so we walked back to The Flat. Missy had her blunt, so she was happy, and she started rolling up the weed as we walked back.

"Can somebody cop our drink for us?" I asked our homeboys. They were sitting on the steps in mixed conversations.

"Can you get me something?" My petty homeboy Mike asked.

"No, Bitch! You can't just get it for us?" I asked in a joking but annoyed tone.

"Nope. I don't like your attitude Bitch, I'm not getting you shit," Mike said as he walked away.

"I'll get it for you. What y'all want?" Marco humbly asked.

"We want Absolut, cranberry juice, 3 cups, and…" I said before he cut me off.

"Wait, if you want all that shit, you need to walk with me," Marco said.

"That's cool. I'll walk with you. I'll be right back y'all," I said to Tesa and Missy. I looked up at Marco and noticed how tall he was, and I liked what I saw. We talked the entire walk to the liquor store. It was a line at the bar, so we stood outside and waited.

"Why are you all dressed up?" he asked.

"I was coming from work. I work in Hunt Valley," I responded.

"Oh, that's a hike. I have a hike to work too. I work in Aberdeen," he said.

"I don't even know where that is, so it must be a hike," I laughed. "So, you are a working man, huh?" I playfully asked.

"Yeah, I been done with that street shit. I might come through and smoke a blunt or something, but for the most part, you can catch my ass clocking in or working a double."

"Well, nice to meet you, Working Man, and thanks for rolling with me to the bar," I said.

"No problem, I can roll with you to some other places too," he said with a dirty smirk.

"No, thanks," I smiled.

We continued to talk as the line slowly moved up. Marco stood behind me, close enough for me to feel he had an erection. I smiled and moved away from his overly excited man piece. I told him my order again, and he walked in to purchase the liquor. When he came back out of the liquor store, he handed me the money back.

"This drink is on me," he said.

"Thanks, Marco. That's What's up. You ready?"

"You have to give me a kiss first," he said with a serious face.

"What? Boy, I don't know you or them lips," I blurted out.

Without saying another word, Marco aggressively grabbed my chin and pulled me close to him and kissed me. I moved my head back, and he pushed my chin away. Marco was aggressive. He did want he wanted to do, and that turned me on. He was also a working man who was not in the streets, which made me admire him. We crossed the road, and when we got on the sidewalk, I grabbed his chin and kissed him as he had done to me, but I bit his lip with force.

"Ouch! Why the fuck you bite my lip? You crazy as shit!" he screamed.

"I do what I want to do, just like you! I bet you don't like me now?" I questioned as I took the lead, walking back to The Flat.

"Shid, I like you more. You are different and crazy. I like crazy!"

"Let's drink to that!" I said.

I cracked open the bottle and poured us both a drink. I watched Marco continue to suck his bottom lip to ease the pain from my bite. That was so funny to me. I didn't know at that very moment that Marco would become a massive part of my life. I didn't think he would give me something to make my heartbeat forever. I wasn't dating anyone, and the timing was perfect for me to be young and spontaneous, well so I thought. We returned to The Flat happy and in our little zone. Tesa wasted no time bitching about how long we took. I ignored her and handed her the already opened liquor bottle.

"Damn, y'all took forever, and you already cracked the shit," Tesa complained.

"Girl chill. Marco bought the drink for us. Here goes your money," I replied as I handed her the money.

"Y'all still took forever," she continued to nag.

"What's up with Marco anyway? We had a nice talk at the bar," I quizzed, completely ignoring her complaints.

"Oh, that's Cousin Marco. He's cool, but he doesn't come around much," Tesa responded in a nonchalant tone.

"Is he your cousin, or are you just calling him Cousin Marco?" I questioned.

"He is actually my cousin, but everyone calls him Cousin Marco too. Hand me the cranberry, please."

I handed Tesa the cranberry juice and continued my drink. I glanced at Marco a few times, and each time we caught eye contact. He pointed at his lip with a frowned face expression as if it were still hurting. I smiled and hunched my shoulders. We continued to smoke weed and drink until I was exhausted. I jumped in my car and dropped off Tesa and Missy before heading home.

About two weeks went by before I ran into Marco again. I was sitting on the steps at The Flat with Missy. He pulled up and rolled down the window of his car. The car was an off-brand car, and it reminded me of a vehicle a cheesy woman would drive. It was a newer car, but I would of much preferred to drive in my Hoopty. I was questioning his character for buying such a vehicle.

"Come here!" Marco yelled from the window.

"Who are you calling Cousin Marco?" Mike asked.

"She knows who I'm calling," he replied as he looked in my direction.

"She? Are you talking to me?" I questioned without budging.

"Stop playing and get in the car," Marco demanded.

"Missy, I'll be back hopefully. He looks kind of crazy," I joked as I walked to Marco's car.

Soon as I got in the car, I questioned why he had such a corny car. He ignored me. I could tell from the way Marco dressed he wasn't materialistic, which was different for me. I wasn't shallow enough to judge a man by his gear, but coming from dealing with a big-time drug dealer, I noticed it. He was dressed neatly, not bad, but just average. It was refreshing to talk to a working man after wearing that black dress to Row's funeral. Marco was safe. He was fun and well respected in the hood, but I didn't have to worry about someone killing him, and that felt comforting.

We drove around and talked. Marco told me he had a female friend he was dealing with, but they had been drifting apart for quite a while. He confessed that we were riding around in her cheesy car. I already knew it was a female's car because there were prissy things all around the car. I saw lip gloss in the middle console, a wig brush on the side door, and mascara on the floor.

Women are incredibly observant, and my eyes traced the car for any sign of a woman soon as I stepped in. Here's where people become fraudulent.

They like to believe that most people they meet don't already have someone or that men are celibate until their beautiful face happens to appear to take them on a love rollercoaster. I never thought that way. Men FUCK! Period! Unless he is practicing celibacy for his religion or some promise he made to himself. Rarely he's waiting for the right one. There is usually always someone in the picture.

I asked no questions about this friend of his. She was not my concern, and we were just taking a ride. I told him I had sex a few times since Row died but wasn't interested in anything serious, and he agreed that he too wasn't looking for a relationship. We continued to talk until we arrived back at The Flat. When I opened the door, he grabbed me.

"I know I just met you, but I like being around you, I'm a come back through here later to see you," Marco said, still holding my arm.

"Okay, I'll see you if I'm still out," I replied.

Soon as he left, I thought of him. I wanted him to come back. I brushed the feeling off because I knew I had only been around him twice, and no way I could be missing him, especially since he had just left. I continued drinking, and before long, I was tore up. I wasn't sloppy like falling all over the place, but my words were slurred. Marco came back, and he was tore up too. He walked right up to me and grabbed my hand. It was a Saturday night, and a lot of people were outside, so his boldness surprised me.

I got up and walked with him. He informed me he missed me too in that short time we had been apart.

"I'm a call you trouble. That's your new name," Marco said, slurring out his words.

"Why am I trouble? What did I do?" I questioned in a joking tone.

"Cause you are going to get me in trouble. You are irresistible. I'm sure you pull your little games on many dudes," he insisted.

"Nope. I be chilling, plus I'm single, and I can do what I want."

"Okay big mouth. You can do what you want? I'm a see if that's true."

We continued to talk as we walked back towards The Flat when suddenly he pulled me into an alley and kissed me roughly. I kissed him back and grabbed his neck as he lifted me off the ground. We passionately kissed. I wrapped my legs around his waist, and he smacked my hand off his neck. I slapped his face, and he looked shocked. I, too, was shocked that I had hit this tall man with broad shoulders. He took his hand and lightly choked my neck as we continued to kiss. I was so wet. Marco was spontaneous, and my girl thumped impatiently, waiting for his boy's arrival.

We could hear people's movements along with faint chatter in the background. My adrenaline was out of control. I was nervous and excited. He took the head of his penis and rubbed it around my girl in a circular motion. I breathed heavy long breaths as if we were already having sex. He was now playing with my clitoris with the head of his penis without ever entering my girl.

"Fuck," he panted, "I don't have a condom on me."

"Shit," I lightly whispered, "why would you tease me like this?" I asked.

"Yeah, you trouble for sure. I think I like trouble," Marco whispered in my ear.

He slowly put me down. He pulled up my pants first and then fixed his clothes. He softly kissed my lips, and we tongue kissed. I instantly respected him. He was clean, and he didn't try to have sex with me unprotected, which turned me on more. He left me with an extremely wet girl, and I left him with an overly excited hard man piece. We both had enough respect for our bodies to leave it at that. I wanted him even more, and he felt the same. We had unfinished business. Our sexual chemistry was out of this world. We were ruff, hard, and uncalculated. He called me two days later. I was so happy when I saw Marco's name pop up on my new pink Razor flip phone.

"Hello, Working Man," I answered in a sexy voice.

"Hey, Trouble. I missed you. Can I be real with you?" Marco asked with hesitation.

"Please do, I expect nothing less," I said in a curious but anxious tone.

"I can't get you out of my mind. Shit be crazy. I'm at work thinking about you and everything."

"Real talk, you been on my mind heavy too, and I don't like it," I admitted.

"Why you don't like it?" he questioned with laughter.

"Because I don't be thinking about no dudes. On top of that, we almost fucked in an alley the other day," I said in a shocked tone.

"Yeah, we were definitely about to fuck like crazy in that alley. Well, I'm not used to women biting me and smacking me and shit. So, this is new for me, too," he chuckled.

"So, what now? I bluntly asked.

"I'm ready for Trouble, that's what's now."

Marco was at my apartment in twenty minutes. I opened the door, and he held up his hand with a box of condoms. We immediately got to it. He talked shit the entire ride to my house about what he was going to do to me and how I would tap out first. I bragged about how he would give in first, and I would leave him sleeping, sucking his thumb. We both talked a lot of trash. I was much younger than Marco, and I knew he had it in his mind that he would have fun with me and then move on with his life. What he didn't predict is how much of a thrill this young woman would be for him.

We fucked the entire night; we had sex until the sun came up. I refuse to let him win, and he held his sex game up for hours. He would ejaculate and take ten-minute breaks, and then he would be ready to go again. I would release and be so relaxed. I'd beg for a ten-minute break, and then I was right back hopping on his boy. As the sunset, we laid in my king-sized bed in a spoon position with his penis still hard in my vagina. I was too competitive to tap out, and he refused to let me win, so we mutually decided to go to sleep with his boy inside me.

We woke up around 10:00 AM to his annoying ring tone. His phone was ringing nonstop. I tapped his shoulder as he snored in a deep sleep, completely ignoring his phone. As he rolled over to silence his phone that sat on my nightstand, his soft penis slowly came out of my vagina.

"I win!" I yelled with a cracking morning voice.

"Shit, well, I need a rematch then," he said, breathing on my neck.

"No rematch. You are not going to be tearing my ass up all the time. I hope I can walk today," I chuckled.

"Girl, you crazy, but for real, I'll be back later for my rematch."

Marco got dressed. I started to say something about who was blowing up his phone, but I felt it wasn't my place. We hadn't even been on a date yet. Whoever was in the picture before me was not my concern. We were just having fun, so I thought. That night Marco came back and the next night and the next night, and the next night, until I looked up one day and realized we were doing more than just having fun, months had passed. We didn't just have sex. We cooked together, talked about our day, watched TV together, rubbed each other's back. We started going out to dinner or catching a movie when he wasn't at work. Every so often, that "friend" would still blow up his phone. I didn't care. I made a promise to myself not to fall in love with anyone after how heartbroken I was from losing Row. As we know, the heart doesn't work like that. I started catching feelings, and so did he. I questioned Tesa about Marco one day while we sat on Oliver Street.

"You know I am dealing with your cousin Marco heavy," I said to Tesa.

"I saw y'all flirting and stuff, but I didn't know y'all was like that," Tesa said with a little sarcasm in her tone.

"Yeah we pass flirting, he's been at my house every night for months, I'm really feeling him," I informed her.

"Oh, I wouldn't get too serious with him, he's not available," Tesa said as she took a hale off her cigarette.

"He told me he had a friend, but they were falling off," I admitted.

"A friend? That's what he told you? Girl, Cousin Marco is married. He has a wife. That's more than a friend," she stated with pleasure in her voice.

"Married? How can a married man stay out every night? You didn't think as my friend you should've told me he was married?" I asked in an angry tone. My feelings were hurt, and it was hard not to show it.

"That wasn't my place," she stated.

"Oh, okay, I know where we stand now. Good to know for you and Marco," I stated as I walked to my car and pulled off.

I was furious with Tesa and Marco. I was only upset with Tesa because of her nasty nonchalant attitude. She was right, it wasn't her place to tell me. I wasn't fucking her. It was Marco's responsibility, to be honest. I called his phone, and he didn't answer, I called back three more times. He finally called me back on his lunch break.

"You married? Really? Fucking married?" I questioned Marco with a loud tone.

"Calm down, Sunni. Stop yelling. I'm a come straight to you after work. We can talk in person," he pleaded with a calm tone.

"Come over? I don't ever want to see you again. You could've been honest and gave me the option to deal with your baggage. I wouldn't have talked to you if I knew you were married," I screamed as tears rolled down my cheeks.

"Wait, you don't even know the situation."

"It doesn't matter what the situation is. You broke the trust, you lied, and you are fucking married, Marco! Married! Married!" I screamed and cried.

"I'll see you tonight, Sunni. We can fix this. Please stop crying. I love you for real. Damn, let's just talk," he pleaded.

"I don't ever want to talk to you again!" I slammed the phone down. I paused for a moment to absorb the fact he just told me he loved me. It was the first time he ever said those words.

I blocked his number, parked my car around the corner from my house so he would think I was out, turned off all the lights, and laid in my bed, and cried. It was nighttime, and I had got used to him being there. I looked forward to our late-night talks, running around the apartment naked, eating snacks on the carpet, and of course, having lots of sex. I couldn't believe he was married, and I couldn't believe how much I had fallen for him. Three days had passed, and not talking to Marco was torture. I didn't even hear him out, but in my mind, it was nothing to be heard. I always thought highly enough of myself to never mess with someone's husband. Why would I want someone's property? I had self-worth. I was young and attractive. My sex game was sick, and my personality was something to miss. In my mind, I didn't need anyone's husband.

On the 4th day, I got dressed to go out to an 80's party. I told myself, *fuck Marco. He got me fucked up, no more crying over his ass.* I put on a cute jean jumper with just a sports bra underneath, some slouch socks, and a pair of high-top Reeboks. I looked real 80's. I put on red lipstick and some colorful bangles. I opened my front door to a tall glass of Marco. I tried to hurry up and shut the door, but he pushed his way through. I panicked because he was right there. It was hard enough avoiding him when he wasn't in my presence, but I knew seeing him in the flesh would be a challenge.

"Please move Marco. I'm about to go out, and I don't have time for this," I stated as I tried to push past the door.

"Why you block me? You not going anywhere until we talk," he said, sternly still blocking the door.

"We don't have shit to talk about. You are married, and I'm single. I don't even like you anymore. Move!" I yelled.

"Really, Sunni. You don't even like me anymore. Come on now," he said as he shut my front door and locked it.

"Come on, what? I don't like you. I don't like liars, and I'm damn sure, not hard up enough to be fucking with someone's husband. Your son you told me about, is that with your wife?" I asked rudely.

"Yeah, that's our son together," he confessed.

"Yuck, you are disgusting. Let me out of my house, please," I said sternly with my nose frowned up at him.

"Sunni, my wife has a boyfriend. We have an open marriage. Why do you think I was able to spend so much time with you? We fell out of love a long time ago. We just have kids to raise and bills to pay together. She deals with her dude, and I deal with you, our spark been dead," he stated.

"I don't believe shit you say out of your mouth anymore. I'm done with you," I said as I tried to push past Marco.

"You are done with me? Huh? You are done with us?" he asked as he roughly grabbed his man piece.

"Yup, fuck y'all. You and your dick."

He roughly pushed me against the wall and unbuckled my jumper. I pushed him off and pulled my jumper back up. He pulled it back down and shoved his tongue in my mouth. I pushed his face with force. He pushed my head against the wall and ripped off my sports bra. He slowly sucked my breast and picked me up. I fought him off until I felt my body fall loosely in his strong arms, and I stop fighting. I kissed him back. He pulled off my jumper, and I stood up against the wall, and he put his entire face in my vagina, and he ate as a bad boy should. I released all over his face. I demanded he got up and finish me. He stood up and pushed me against the wall and jammed his penis in my anxiously awaiting vagina. I smacked his face over and over again as tears ran down my cheeks.

"I'm sorry I hurt you, I'm so sorry, I love you," he whispered in my ear as he stroked deeper in my vagina.

"I hate you," I whispered as I continued to cry quietly.

"No, you don't. We will fix this. I promise," Marco whispered as he gently stroked his penis in and out as we stood on the wall at the front door. I said nothing. I felt so confused. My chemistry with Marco was undeniable. I was already in too deep. I was in love with a married man.

I loved Marco before I knew he was married, and unfortunately, my heart didn't give a fuck he was married. My mind cared, and so did my pride, oh, and my self-esteem cared too, but my heart and my hot ass vagina wanted Marco. So, they won. I treated Marco like pure shit for months. It didn't stop him from coming around or laying his pipe in my walls. He didn't give up. I stop talking about his marriage; it was pointless. I didn't tell my family right away about Marco's little secret, but I did vent to one of my closest co-workers.

"Can I tell you something? It's killing me inside," I asked Tasha as I picked up some papers from the table.

"Sure. You know how we talk, girl," Tasha replied.

"Marco is married. I tried to leave him alone, but I'm too gone. I know that sound like an excuse, but...," I stopped talking as Tasha's face expression was frowned up, and she looked angry.

"But what? There is no but's Sunni. Just leave him alone!" Tasha stated with aggression.

"Much easier said than done, Tasha."

"No, it's real easy. You know I'm somebody's wife too. I would try to kill a homewrecker like you. I hate a woman who doesn't respect other people vows," she stated as she snatched the stapler.

"Why is it my job to respect his vows? He should respect his own commitment that he made to his wife. Why must I be loyal to his wife? I didn't promise her sickness and health to death do us part," I bluntly said.

"You also know he's not on the market for you to play with like your personal toy. He belongs to someone!" Tasha yelled. Everyone in the office turned to look at us.

"Why are you getting loud? We are both victims. Me and her. Which apparently, she has a boyfriend anyway, but besides that. Why is the woman always so angry at the woman? I was single, and he was not. He disrupted my peaceful life, as well. It's not my job to be the marriage police and watch out for every married woman's fake committed husband."

"It is your job as a woman. It's called respect Sunni. Respect for other people's marriage. How would their child feel if they got divorced because of you?"

"Not because of me, but because of a decision their father made. I don't have the power to ruin a family; only the cheater can ruin his own family. I didn't wake up and say, "Oh, I'm a fuck someone's husband today," It happened, and I later found he was married."

"Well, once you knew he was married, you should've ended it right away. What if your husband did that to you, how would you feel?" Tasha asked as she picked up her stack of papers from the copy machine.

"I would be angry with my husband for breaking our trust. Fuck the woman! She wouldn't owe me shit. My husband would be the one who promised me respect, and he would have to pay," I said as I snatched up my papers.

"I'm disappointed in you, Sunni," Tasha stated with a look of disgust.

"Well, be disappointed. I wish I never said anything," I replied in a defensive tone.

"I wish you never said anything too!" Tasha stated as she walked away.

This marriage topic was the beginning of the judgment. I went to the woman's bathroom at work and cried. I felt like pure shit after my talk with

Tasha. She made me feel worthless. I felt like I needed to explain to her how it happened and that I didn't know he was married at first. I needed to explain how we dated for months before I knew. Actually, I didn't need to explain shit. Who the fuck was she? Who the fuck were all those people who judged me? Being away from Marco made me unhappy. Being with Marco made me happy. So, I went with happiness. I utterly understood the song, "If Loving You Is Wrong, I Don't Want To Be Right."

Once I stop obsessing about the marriage issue. Marco and I had a much bigger topic to discuss. This was an issue that wouldn't go away, and divorce papers couldn't help. We often look at issues in life in a negative light. We rarely look at life as a solution; instead, everything is always a problem. There are no problems in life, only solutions because we are here to experience life, and there is an answer to every question. Marco's marriage didn't break us, but this phone call would.

"Hey Marco, how was work?" I asked.

"It was cool. I'm tired as shit. You cooking later?" Marco asked.

"I don't know my appetite been crazy. I need to tell you something tonight," I said in a frightful tone.

"I don't like how you sound. Tell me now," Marco demanded.

"It can wait until tonight. Are you coming here or going home?"

"I do need to go home and get more clothes. Did you wash clothes, yet? If so, I can come straight to you. But anyway, tell me what's wrong before I get there."

"Yeah, I washed clothes. Okay, I'll just say it. I missed my period. I have a pregnancy test in front of me, which reads positive," I blurted out. Marco got quiet. All I heard was him breathing on the phone.

"For real?" he asked with no emotion.

"Yes, for real. I have been nauseated in the morning too. I'm quite sure it's the real deal."

"How you want to handle this? You know I don't want any more kids, and I know you talked of big dreams for yourself," Marco said.

"I'm 19, and I definitely want to travel the world, but it's a person growing inside of me, and I kind of want to meet it," I softly said.

"You know I love you, Sunni, but a child is not what I want. I have four kids, and I'm just starting to have freedom. You sure you ready to give up all your freedom too?"

"I'm not sure about anything. All I know is, I've never been pregnant before. I feel different, and I want to meet this little person. That's all I'm sure of," I admitted.

"So, fuck what I have to say? Are you making your own decisions now? It should be both of our decision!" Marco yelled.

"Calm down. Listen, if you want out, that's cool. Let me remind you that we both knew I wasn't on birth control, and we both fucked raw. We only talked about kids once when I first met you. So, don't act like this is a trap. I promise you I will carry this decision on my own but don't act like you are a victim."

"So, your mind is made up? Is that what you're telling me?" he asked with irritation.

"Yup, I'm having this baby with or without you. Maybe you shouldn't come over tonight. Go home to your family," I sarcastically stated.

"Really, Sunni! So, you about to be on your bullshit. I'm not running or leaving you alone. I just think you are not being fair."

I hung up the phone, it was nothing more to say. I call this period, "The shift." Everything changed, including Marco. I watched my body grow in a way I could never imagine. My eating habits changed, and so did my other patterns. There was no more partying or drinking. I even had to stop smoking weed. My mornings were hell for the first three months. Marco held my hair as I would slump over the toilet, gagging my brains out. Marco wasn't excited about the baby, which caused a rain on my parade. I was overly excited. I looked at baby clothes every day. I already knew what kind of stroller and car seat I wanted. I was baby obsessed. I couldn't wait to find out the gender. I wanted a boy. Some appointments Marco attended and some appointments he was a no show. At first, I was disappointed, but then I started not to care.

This brisk winter day was such a good day. It was the day I found out if I was having a boy or a girl. Marco was secretly hoping for a girl. He mentioned a time or two how a little girl would be nice. I laid on the doctor's table as he put a cold blue jelly substance all over my belly. I heard the heartbeat and smiled with joy. That was my favorite part of all my prenatal visits; I could listen to the heartbeat. My doctor was an older white man named Dr. Smiller. His hands would shake sometimes, and I wondered if he should still be delivering babies or had he passed the retirement age. I decided to keep him as my doctor because he made me comfortable, so I disregarded his age. I sat on the table anxiously waiting.

"Okay Sunni. Let's see what we have here," Dr. Smiller stated.

"Yes, I'm so excited. Please be a boy, please be a boy," I whispered as he moved the tool around my stomach looking for the baby's private area.

"Well, Ms. Sunni, I'm proud to tell you..." he stopped mid-sentence.

"Tell me what? Please tell me! You killing me, Dr. Smiller," I asked anxiously.

"I'm proud to tell you that you are having a beautiful little boy."

"Yes! Whoop. I can't wait to meet you, my beautiful son. I knew it was a boy—my little son. I already have your name, baby. I can't wait to meet you," I screamed with joy as I talked to my big belly. I called Marco soon as I left out of the doctor's office.

"Marco, It's a boy!" I hollered with excitement.

"Oh word, that's what's up," he said with no emotion. His tone was low and unbothered.

"Oh, okay. Well, have a good day," I said with disappointment as I hurried up and hung up the phone. His tone killed my vibe, and I made my mind up right there to have my baby alone.

I ignored Marco. I ignored his calls, text, emails, and even ignored him when he came to my house unexpectedly. I was so in love with my unborn child that anyone who didn't feel the same way would be immediately cut, including his father. I stop telling him about my doctor's visits. I was seven months pregnant, and Marco called one day upset after I hadn't seen him for about a month.

"About time you answered the phone. What the fuck is up?" Marco asked with agitation.

"Hi, to you too, Marco. Everything is good. I'm just getting everything together for my little king.

How you been?" I asked while putting sheets in the crib.

"I'm good. How is he? Is he growing good and everything? I miss y'all so much. You just cut me off, like I was nothing."

"Yup, he's growing beautifully. He's highly active in my belly," I snickered. "It's not that I cut you off. You made it clear you didn't want to be involved. I know you tried, but it wasn't genuine. It was best this way."

"What way? He's coming now Sunni, so it doesn't matter what I felt at first, I'm here."

"It kind of matters to me because I'm so in love with him that he deserves the same amount of excitement from you too. Anyway, do you want to know his name?"

"Sure. Just know I'm still here for you."

"His name will be Zi Connor. Do you like it?"

"The first name is different and unique, but you are not giving him my last name?" he asked with frustration.

"Uhm, No, Marco. You were against my decision, you are married, and he's my baby so he will carry my father's last name."

"That's bullshit, and I don't agree with your dumb ass..." he continued to curse before I hung up.

I might have been young and stupid with the married situation, but no one, I meant no one was going to play with my son. The last two months were hard. I couldn't even tie my shoes anymore. My ankles were swollen, and I had gained 50 pounds. My breasts were plump and full. I stared in the mirror at my chest and prayed I could keep them. It was the one body enhancement that I liked. I was ready for this little human to evacuate my body. My baby and I were extremely close even while he lived inside of me. He rolled his hand against my skin, and I could count his knuckles. That always amazed me. I loved sharing my body with him. I felt complete.

I worked my job up until the day I went into labor. My king was coming, and I awaited his arrival. I decided not to have any medication during childbirth. I wanted a natural birth. What a damn fool I was. I was in excruciating pain. I pushed out an 8.2-ounce baby boy with a head full of hair. He was perfect. When Dr. Smiller handed me, my son, I was in disbelief that he belonged to me. He was gorgeous, and everyone noticed. He was the cutest baby in the nursery, and all the nurses complimented me on how handsome he was. Newborns can be funny looking but not my king. He came out with his features ready for the world. Marco held our son and gazed in his eyes; he looked at me and said, "He's beautiful, Sunni. Thanks for keeping him." I just smiled. Now I have found unconditional love. Now I have something to live for. Now I can breathe, now I can look forward to life, now my heart can beat.

CHAPTER 4

FREAKING OFF THE ECSTASY WAY

(Freaking Off: Having sex for money with people, you know. You share a common attraction with the person, but they ain't shit, so you charge them for sex. Not to be confused with prostitution.)

(Ecstasy: A street drug in the form of a pill known as an E Pill which gives you a high of freedom)

After giving birth to Zi, everything changed. I had to share my new world with this little person who depended on me. Marco instantly fell in love with our son from the moment he laid eyes on his precious face. I lost something for Marco during my pregnancy. I had sex with him from time to time but nothing like before. I lost feelings from his lack of support. The rejection turned me off. Marco admired me more after seeing what kind of loving mother I was. It was like he was more attracted to me than before I had Zi. I no longer wanted to pursue a relationship with him. I suggested we co-parent, and he eventually agreed.

I experienced some embarrassing changes as well, like leaking milk from my breast in a crowded store. No one informed me my breasts would leak. I had to find out the hard way with two big wet milk circles covering my nipples in a crowded Walmart. Postpartum depression was real. I envisioned I would have my body right back after giving birth. My stomach was black like street tar and wrinkled like an elephant's ass. My six-pack was gone, and the sight of my new stomach was disturbing. I did enjoy my fresh boobs that were full and perfectly shaped; however, they were sore all the time and leaked. I was also depressed that Zi was outside of my body. I felt alone again. I enjoyed growing a human inside of me. I knew he was right there in the flesh, but I missed him being with me all the time in the wound.

I was 20 years old and living like an old ass woman. I went to work and came home to motherhood. I hung out sometimes, but that always included a stroller and a car seat, which wasn't too fun. There was no greater joy than having my son. He put a spark in my eyes that I had lost during my trauma years. My son was exactly what I needed, and every touch from his little fingers gave me a burst of happiness. I was obsessed.

Months had passed, and life threw me a blessing, which included freedom. My freedom saver was my father. He had been released from prison, and he came to stay with Zi and I. During this time, my father was a complete disaster. He was always coming home, bruised up from falling off his motorcycle. He regularly snuck women in the house. Imagine that, a father sneaking women into his daughter's house. He made messes that I was forced to clean up, and to be frankly honest, he was a pain in my ass. Although my father was a walking disaster, we had so much fun while he lived there. We watched movies, cooked dinner together, and played games.

He loved his grandson so much, and he offered to watch him so I could live my life a little. Soon as he would suggest that he could watch him, I left the house so fast, smoke would come from my shoes. Those few hours of freedom was what I needed. On this weird night, I woke up in the middle of the night with an excruciating urge to pee. I opened my bedroom door and stepped onto something fluffy, and I saw a mist of white sprinkles of something floating in the air.

"Daddy! What happened in here?" I yelled as I walked in the direction of the bathroom.

"Girl, what are you screaming about in the middle of the damn night?" he asked in a groggy tone.

"Daddy, it's white stuff everywhere. Why are you hiding behind the door? What happened in there?" I asked as I approached his bedroom door.

"I'm your father. Don't question me. Take your ass back to bed. Good night Sunni!" he yelled from the door.

"No, not good night, Daddy. It's morning! Open the door!" I demanded standing outside of the bedroom door.

"Girl, you are a pain in my ass! We can talk in the morning," he said as he peeked out the crack of the bedroom door.

"Nope, let's talk now. It's a damn mess out here," I shouted as I pushed the bedroom door open. The room looked as if it had snowed inside the house.

"Shit, I was going to get it up before you woke up."

"What the hell happened in here, Daddy?" I questioned as I looked around with a look of confusion.

"Something was crawling in the futon, so I took my knife and started cutting it open to kill whatever it was," he explained while moving his hands to show me how he butchered my futon.

"What was crawling, Daddy? What was crawling? Nothing was crawling Daddy. You know what, just never mind," I said as I shut the door and walked to the bathroom.

"I'm a clean it up Baby Girl, and I will buy you a new one. I'm a replace the comforters too! I promise," he yelled from the closed door.

My father murdered my futon, the comforters, and the pillows while he was on a butchering spree trying to kill nothing. He knew he had to kiss up, so he offered to watch Zi for the weekend. It was also a secure method to shut me up. I happily accepted. Fuck the death of the futon. I was hitting the streets, and I couldn't wait to be free. Later that night, I got dressed and called up Missy to meet me on Oliver Street at Sherry's bar. We got tore up, and 2:00 AM came fast. We wanted to catch the bar on Biddle Street before they closed, so we left Sherry's a little early.

"Damn, it's live out here. I can't believe it's 2 o'clock already. I'm trying to stay out for real," I said to Missy with excitement.

"You trying to pop? That's what I had. My ass is up," Missy asked.

"Pop what? An E Pill?" I questioned as I walked in the line at the bar.

"Yeah. It's an upper. We can keep the party going!"

"Bitch. I never popped before. How will I feel? I don't want to be all high and stupid," I confessed.

"You know I'm a keep it real with you. The pill will have you up all night. You may get extremely horny. Your hands will sweat when it starts to kick in, and cigarettes will taste like butter," Missy explained as we got closer to our turn in the line to order the drinks.

"Sounds good to me. I knew it was a party high, but I was always scared to try new shit. Where can we get them from?"

"We have to go up the hill. You only need half; just save the other half for the next time you want to be up."

I popped an E Pill called "Naked Lady." I didn't feel anything for the first five minutes except the alcohol I had already consumed. Then, my hands got sweaty, and everything looked more beautiful. The streetlights were brighter, and the music in the car sounded so much better. The high was kicking in. My eyes were glassy, and I felt a sense of ease come over me. I felt so free. My mind calmed down, and all thoughts of responsibility left. My throat was dry. It seemed as if Missy could read my mind because, at that very moment, she handed me a bottle of water. We drove to an After-Hour club over West Baltimore. She rolled a blunt and threw the guts from the blunt paper out the window.

"Don't be throwing shit out the window! Give me a hale off that cigarette," I yelled over the music.

"Here. Don't you have that Jeezy CD? Put that shit on!" Missy said as she handed me the cigarette.

"Yup, you know I got it. Damn, I feel so good friend," I said with excitement.

"I knew you would. How do you feel, though? You don't feel crazy or nothing, right?" Missy asked.

"Not crazy at all. I feel the horny side effect, though. I can't believe how good this cigarette taste either. You know I usually only take a hale here and there when I'm drunk, but I want this whole cigarette," I said in amazement.

I admired the fresh air hitting my face as we drove with all the windows down with the stereo at the highest volume. We sang along with every song that played. The ecstasy made me drive calmer than if I was drunk from alcohol. I let the car float and drive itself. By now I was on my 5th car, I had a baby blue Cadillac Deville with an all-white interior, with custom made Cadillac signs on each seat. The car caused a lot of attention. Men often stopped me at the traffic lights to say things like, "Damn that baby hard as shit." They always assumed it was a male's car because most women wouldn't want such a big car. The Cadillac also caused negative attention from the police. They consistently pulled me over, assuming it was a drug dealer's car. It was a beauty and a headache.

We arrived at the After-Hour club, and I was relieved to park the car. I was happy we made it there safe. We walked up to the front door to pay our $20 to get in. All the girls who stood outside frowned their faces at us, and all the guys admired us. Missy and I were the same type of girl far as looks go. We didn't look alike, but we were both attractive, slim with a long face shape. Usually, it was a matter of preference; if a guy liked a darker female than he would go for Missy, but if he wanted a lighter female, than I would be his preference. I loved surrounding myself with attractive females, they were less envious. They had confidence and less drama. Not that I went out my way to only befriend attractive women, it just so happens they were the ones I clicked with.

We had fun at the After Hour, we left around 5:00 in the morning. The high was still there with a full force, and although it was the next morning, we were wide awake. We drove back over East with the music still blasting. We decided to go back to the bar on Biddle Street to get more drinks as it was just opening, which reminded me it was a new morning. We ran into a guy named Richard that Missy knew. Richard was dark, slim, and had no noticeable attractive features. He was a decent looking guy but not appealing enough for me to remember. He parked his pickup truck as he hopped out in his work clothes.

"Missy! What's up, girl?" Richard yelled across the street as he looked both ways to cross the street.

"Ain't shit. Why are you outside so early?" Missy asked.

"I just worked a double. What are y'all doing out so early?" Richard questioned while glaring at us with flirty eyes.

"Shit, we are just out. Buy us a drink." Missy demanded in an aggressive tone.

"You got that. She's cute. What's her name?" Richard asked Missy.

"I'm right here. Why not ask me my name? I'm Sunni," I said to Richard.

"Nice to meet you, Sunni. I'm trying to hang out with y'all beautiful ladies. What y'all want to drink?"

"Absolut and cranberry are cool. Thanks, Richard, nice to meet you too," I said to Richard as I watched him walk in the liquor store.

"Girl, he will pay to fuck. You still horny? What are you trying to do?" Missy whispered to me.

"How much? Yup, still horny. We mind as well make this a night to remember," I said in a low tone.

"A couple hundred at least. Yup, we can bank his ass real quick," Missy said as she looked in his direction.

"I want a couple hundred by myself, not to share. I'll do the negotiating. No gay shit, though. Just us doing him," I stated.

"You know I don't fuck with no Bitches. Ok yeah, you do all the talking," Missy said as she nodded to inform me, he was coming towards us.

"Ok, but it's cool to smack my ass or touch a boob or something. We have to give him some kind of thrill," I whispered with laughter.

"Y'all never said what y'all was about to do," Richard said as he walked upon us, handing us the drinks.

"We about to do you! Both of us!" I boldly said.

"Do me? I'm not that lucky. I would give my whole paycheck to have two pretty ladies like y'all," Richard stated.

"The whole paycheck sounds good to me. How it sounds to you, Missy?" I asked with a smirk.

"Sound hella good to me too," Missy agreed.

"For real? Y'all playing and shit. I got $200 if y'all serious."

"We are serious, but we want $400 apiece," I said to Richard as I pulled my drink in the clear plastic cup.

"Damn, that's too much, Babe. I still have to eat," Richard said.

"No problem. You just missed out on the thrill of your life. Thanks for the drinks, Richard. Come on, Missy," I said as I prepared to cross the street.

"Wait! Damn. I got it. Let's go have some fun."

We left with Richard, and he drove straight to the ATM and withdrew $700 and handed it to us. He shorted us both $50 apiece, we cursed at him before we let it go. Richard and Missy made small talk as we drove to his house. I didn't know the people they were speaking of, so I remained quiet. Richard lived at home in his mama's basement. Had I known he lived at home; I would have asked for much more. This adventure wasn't really about the money anyway, it was about the experience. We were being spontaneous and having fun. Sex came with the high, so why not get a few dollars in the process? Richard immediately dropped his clothes. To my surprise, he had a well-built body under his work clothes. Richard had a six-pack and a generous sized hard penis. He laid on the bed ass naked, waiting for us to catch up. Missy and I slowly got undressed. I glanced at her nude body, and she glanced at mines. I felt no attraction to a woman, and I could tell she didn't feel anything either. I walked over to the bed.

"Come on, ladies. Can y'all suck it?"

"We told you in the car, no oral sex for you or between us. Don't worry, you will get pleased, Baby," I said in a sexy tone in the hopes of shutting down his request.

I walked over and slowly jerked his man piece, which had gradually gone down from the disappointment of no head. Missy spit on it as I jerked. He moaned and requested Missy to get on his dick. Missy slid the condom on his dick and looked at me with fear in her eyes. I wasn't sure if it was the size that frightened her or going first, but I decided to take one for the team. I got on his hard-hot penis and slowly slid down. For a split moment, I had forgotten that it was a financial arrangement as I enjoyed riding his wood. I was lost in the ecstasy, and I secretly enjoyed every stroke. Missy reminded me of where I was by smacking my ass. Then I looked at Richard's moaning face, which wasn't so cute from that angle, and I remembered that we were freaking off. I hopped off his penis and motioned for Missy to get on. She instead bent over and arched her back.

"Ride it for me. Ride this dick Missy," Richard demanded.

Missy looked at me with irritation as Richard's demands were getting annoying. She obliged and got on his dick to ride it. He pumped her hard and deep. She glanced at me, and I smacked her ass to cheer her on as she had done to me. He moaned, and I played with his balls as she continued to ride him.

"Come on, bend over!" Richard demanded.

"I have to go to the bathroom. It's Sunni's turn," Missy said with a sneaky smirk on her face as she slowly walked up the basement steps to find the bathroom.

Missy going to the bathroom was the beginning of her shenanigans. She made any excuse to run from the dick. She had to call her grandmother, she needed some water, the liquor made her dizzy, the room was too dark, she got a cramp in her toe. Her excuses were ridiculous. Richard took many breaks to avoid ejaculating. I was sick of his ass. He had stamina, and I was tired of his overly hard dick. I pushed him on the bed, and I bent over doggy style. I knew talking dirty along with no breaks, he was sure to release.

"Stop playing with me. You like to play with this pussy? Let that nut out, Baby," I said as I grabbed his waist and roughly fucked him as he hit from the back.

Richard came instantly and fell to the bed in exhaustion. I was so relieved he released. We washed up, and Richard drove us back to my car. He begged to do it again soon. We played along, but we knew that would never happen again. I was finally getting tired, and the high was slowly wearing off.

"Bitch, you really owe me some of your money. You hardly did anything!" I said to Missy.

"I'm sorry, friend. I didn't mean to keep leaving you. He was taking forever," she laughed.

"You not funny! I was sick of his ass too!"

"I know. I won't ever leave you hanging like that again. Tell the truth, we underestimated Richard's ass, didn't we?" Missy asked.

"Hell yeah! That mother fucker can go. He had dick control, and I wasn't expecting his penis to be that big."

"That's what we get for trying to be out here selling pussy like we know what we were doing. Talking about we going to have an adventurous night and shit," Missy laughed.

"Yeah, all highed up! If I ever do this again, I have questions. I need to see the size and put a time limit on that shit," I chuckled.

I drove home in deep thought. I giggled to myself while reminiscing about the night we had. When I was 16, I tried to sell pussy for some school clothes, and the guy snuck off the condom and left me with a burning vagina. I said I would never do anything like that again, yet here I was living on the edge. For me, ecstasy was just a party high. It was not an everyday drug like weed. I would never want to be that high every day. My relationship with drugs was always stern. I had no interest in experimenting with anything more than weed. My childhood molded me to hate drugs. I knew exactly how they could destroy a life. Luckily for me, ecstasy was not that kind of drug.

Things work differently in the hood. There are 3 main categories of women and 2 types of men. Category #1 is the women who are at home being wifey material, although they usually don't have a ring. They have significant responsibilities. They have to bail out their drug dealer boyfriends, stay up all night and worry when he's out fucking and sucking. Call the jails looking for him when he doesn't come home. Pay for his funeral if he happened to get killed. Lastly, she takes care and watches all his children, even the ones that are not hers.

Category #2 is the side chick. She really loves the guy. She doesn't get any holidays with him, and she has to wait for his every move. She doesn't have to bail him out or bury him. She gets to fuck him, spend his money, and send him home. She sometimes dates other men, but usually, she is loyal to the one guy that is not available. Her feelings are often hurt, and she continuously fights for attention from a man that is not hers.

Category #3 is a true single woman. She can do and date whoever she wants. Her loyalty is with no one. She is single. She can have a sugar daddy, date other single people, sell pussy, meet guys online, have threesomes, or whatever she wants. Most holidays she will spend alone, she won't have the responsibilities of the Wifey or the side chick. She can charge a fee to both of their men (since they share) and move on with her life. No feelings, no attachments, just business. Also, in this category are the freaks, they just fuck everyone for free.

The two types of men in the hood are either the working man or the drug dealer. They both are liable to cheat. The working man usually cheats less, if at all. He can have an around the way chick too that he's been dealing with for years. The drug dealer is almost a guarantee cheater. In the streets, it's so much opportunity for pussy. You got the block chicks, the side chicks, the freaks, the pussy selling chicks, the young chicks, and the list goes on. It's nightlife, and shit happens. It comes with the game. No judgment on either type of woman or man in the hood. Before one can be so quick to judge, they should always count their partners over the years. The numbers add up quickly. And for those who want to feel like they are better or so innocent, you know the ones who will read this and say, "I only slept with 2 men my entire life!" Good for you, but I hate to tell you Wifey, "You've been cheated on by one of the above categories."

I fell under category #3. I was single, and I did what the fuck I wanted to do unapologetically. For the most part, I was home, cooking, cleaning, and being a mother. When I wasn't being a mother is when I allowed my wild side to conquer me. These wild nights were far and few in between. Maybe once a month at the most, the other 29 days of the month, I was being good and working. I didn't search for male attention. I had a father who loved me dearly. I knew I didn't want a committed relationship, so men were only good for sex and money. Let me explain how my wild nights took a turn for the worse.

I picked up my son from Courts housing development. Marco's aunt Mae watched Zi while I worked. I came out of the building and saw Missy walking across the street. She noticed Zi and walked up to us. She kissed Zi all over his cheeks, and he blushed with laughter.

"Hey, Zi Zi. Dag, he's getting big," Missy said to Zi as she took him out of my arms.

"I know, right. What are you doing down here?" I asked as I looked in Zi's baby bag for a wipe.

"Shit. I'm at my best friend's house in the other court. I'm coming from getting some blunts from the store."

"Oh, Tesa lives down here now?" I asked.

"No. I'm talking about my best friend Felicia, but we call her Licia. It's about to rain, come around her house with me, and we can smoke real quick."

"Damn, you talked the rain up. It's coming down hard!" I said as we ran to Licia's house in the pouring down rain. Missy covered Zi and ran with him on her side. I grabbed the stroller and ran behind them.

We were drenched in a matter of two minutes. Zi laughed uncontrollably, I guess he had fun in the rain. We walked through the building to Licia's apartment. Missy opened the door without knocking and held it for me to enter. The apartment had a party vibe. I could smell the weed in the air, and there were empty bottles of liquor on the tables.

"Licia, this my homegirl Sunni and her son Zi," Missy announced.

"How are you doing? Y'all really got caught in the rain. I have something for your son to put on to get him out of those wet clothes. Hold up," Licia said as she walked to the back of her apartment.

"She seems cool. This where you be at now?" I asked Missy.

"Yeah, she cool as shit. I be down here sometimes."

"Here you go. So, you smoke?" Licia asked as she handed me an outfit for Zi."

"You know damn well if she be with me then she smokes," Missy yelled out.

"Oh, ard. Your son can go in the play pin with my son while we smoke if you want," Licia said.

"Thank you. How many kids do you have?" I asked Licia.

"Two. A boy and a girl. Missy turn that song up!" Licia said to Missy referring to Little Wayne song "The Sky Is The Limit." We all sung along.

"And you know that I'm a ride for my motherfuckin n*ggas. Most likely I'm a die with my finger on the trigger. Don't worry bout mine, I'm a grind till I get it. And tell all of my n*ggas that the sky is the limit - The sky is the limit."

Felicia and I clicked immediately. Her home became my second home. Licia was a cute brown-skinned girl with chinky eyes, she wore her hair in a short cut. Her personality was quiet, especially when she was high. She could hold a decent conversation, but she was laid back. She would never be the loudest girl in the room. It was the summer of 2007; it was a summer we would always remember. I started going to Licia's house every day after work. I picked up Zi and walked to her court, and the fun would begin. I rarely went straight home. At first, I just went over to smoke weed and have a drink. Things quickly changed when the "Naked Lady" (E Pill) showed up. Oh, the "Naked Lady" was a feisty Bitch, and she would get us in a whole lot of trouble. Her friends weed, and alcohol sure didn't help the situation.

Licia's house allowed me freedom as a mother. My son was welcomed, and we were always mothers first. We took our children to places like Disney On Ice, Chuck E Cheese, or just to the park. We made sure they had fun. Licia helped her daughter with her homework every day after school, and she cooked dinner every night. Our kids became best friends, and I found myself hanging with Licia more than Missy. I was a working woman, a mother, a friend, and a provider during the day. The freaks do come out at night, and we undoubtedly participated in the nighttime freaking.

We partied like Rock Stars on the weekends. There was no such thing as a boring weekend. We sometimes got high, and we sometimes freaked off. Freaking off doesn't mean we had sex with strangers every weekend. It's a very random act that usually occurs when you are incredibly high and with other high people. Freaking off also doesn't mean you're a hoe or slut. Freaking off is two people who are attracted to each other, sexually or physically, and the man pays to have sex with the woman. Why is money involved? Why not just have sex with a person you are attracted to? Why charge for something both parties want to do? It's simple. It's the game of pay to play. When money is involved, so are rules. Since the guy paid, he is allowed secrecy and the freedom to play without the consequences. Unlike a side chick who usually catch feelings and cause problems at the guy's home and unlike a freak who just fuck everyone for free, so her vagina has no value. For me freaking off was random and something I did spontaneously.

These men that pay to play are not the kind of men I would desire as a mate. They are men I would only fuck for a price. They are not husband material. Why would I think with that mindset? I'll tell you why! I grew up in poverty, and everything must have value. The value could be love, feelings, or money. I either loved you, and we were in a committed relationship, or I fucked you for a fee. When I was in a relationship, I was an angel. I never stepped out or cheated. I was always content with one man. In a relationship, love would be the value. When I was single and had no interest in feelings, then money would be the value. I didn't want to lay on my back with a dog to get a wet ass just for pleasure.

Ecstasy was taking over the city, and it was the perfect party drug to stay up and fuck. There was a serious problem with ecstasy penis! It could go all night. It could be torture. If a guy was too high, he might experience limp dick, but that didn't stop him from trying. It would be a tedious process from hard to limp and back hard again. It was an annoying side effect of the E Pill for some men. Let me tell you something, the men that didn't get limp dick would literally kill you from his stamina. Either way, if I was sober, I had no interest in having sex with a guy high off ecstasy. It would be a headache, and I would want him to ejaculate and get the fuck off of me. Since I too was high when these transactions took place, it was a thrill of a lifetime. I had the energy and the wetness to keep up with an ecstasy dick.

Licia and I partied like no tomorrow. We blasted the music, ate crabs, smoked weed, and got drunk. We sometimes played cards, usually spades, and we talked trash. I sold marijuana, and Licia allowed me to get weed sales from her house. I never missed work, and I rarely popped an E pill during the week. The summer was coming to an end, and my body was tired. Licia and I sat in her living room and watched Family Feud.

"Licia, how you feel?" I asked.

"Friend, I feel tired. We've been up two days straight. How you feel?" Licia asked.

"I'm burnt out. My body is burnt out too. I have no energy, and I feel weak for real," I said as I laid across the sofa, smoking a blunt.

"Damn. It's like you read my mind. I feel the same way," Licia agreed.

"After this weekend, I'm done with the E pills. We both need to be done for real."

"Hell yeah! I'm done too. But look, let's finish rocking this weekend out," Licia suggested.

"That's cool. We mind as well stay up the whole weekend. But you must admit we rocked this summer out. We had a freaking ball!" I said with excitement.

"You ain't never lied," Licia chuckled.

We went to Licia's neighbor, Destiny apartment, and had the time of our lives. We popped an E, and we sweated. We danced, laughed, loudly sung songs, and lived in the moment. It was a moment of wildness, freedom, and just not giving a fuck. Licia and I lived that summer exactly how we wanted. Our reckless behavior only lasted that summer. The memories would last a lifetime. It was the summer of 2007 that we named "Freaking Off The Ecstasy Way." Where the dicks stayed super hard, the nights lasted super long, and the memories would last a lifetime.

CHAPTER 5

I KNEW BETTER

I knew better! I could've easily played dumb like I didn't know any better. I should've listened to everyone who preached about how wrong I was. I knew this decision would one day come to bite me in the ass. I didn't think I would have to pay for a lifetime. I regrettably must own my shit. I fucked up, and I can't blame anyone but myself because the truth is, I fucking knew better!

After the summer down Licia's house, I went back to the normal boring mother I originally was. I still hung out on occasions, but I started working more and partying less. My father moved out of my apartment into his own place. He started working at a mechanic shop on the other side of town, so we didn't see him as much. Zi and I missed his presence around the house. I didn't miss the occasional floating feathers in the middle of the night, but I would be lying if I said we didn't miss him dearly. Zi often looked for his Pop-Pop.

So, here's the dull day that meant nothing to me until it meant something to me. I went on Oliver street with Missy to hang out. I went inside Sherry's Bar and played music on the jukebox. I sat at the bar and ordered a shot of Absolut Vodka. I talked to the old heads who sat at the bar for hours talking about pensions and how completely fucked this Country is with all the new rules. I usually joined in with my two sense. I loved joking and talking trash with the old men. I talked a lot of junk, and they bought me a lot of drinks.

I decided to go back outside to see who was on the block. I bumped into a guy named Kells. I knew him from The Flat from years prior, but I never really held a conversation with him. We just casually spoke to each other. I thought he was mean, and I didn't like his persona. I kept my distance. Kells was thick with a dark caramel complexion. He had a charming smile with an adorable dimple, a little pop belly, and his eyes showed a lot of expressions. All I knew about Kells from The Flat was that he was an amazing father. He always kept his two kids with him, and I admired that side of him. I still thought his attitude sucked. I was rushing out of the bar, and I had my head turned when I pumped into him.

"My bad," I said to Kells.

"It's cool. What's up?" he asked looking directly in my eyes.

"Ain't shit. What's up with you?" I asked out of courtesy.

"Nothing, about to grab these blunts. You smoking?" Kells asked as he looked at a car riding by.

"Nah, I'm good. Thanks, though," I stated as I walked pass.

I continued my night and thought nothing of the conversation until the next time I came outside to hang. Missy kept telling me Kells was asking about me. I was confused about where his sudden attraction for me came from, and honestly, I had no interest in finding out. Later that night, one of my homeboys informed me Kells was looking for me. I was confused once again. I ran into Kells a few times, and he expressed how he was feeling me. I thought Kells was a grump and I avoided him as much as possible until this one day. He stood right outside the bar as I came out, and there was nowhere for me to go.

"What's up? Why are you playing? I know Missy told you I been trying to get at you," Kells said as he broke up the weed to put it in a blunt.

"I'm not playing. She mentioned something. Anyway, what's up?" I asked with irritation.

"I've been trying to get your number and see what's up with you."

"Oh, I was confused about where this sudden interest in me came from. You can put my number in your phone."

I gave Kells my number, and he called the next night. He asked to take me out for the weekend, and I agreed. I had no intention of going out with him. I stood him up. I didn't answer the phone when he called, nor did I feel bad for standing him up. After doing some research on Kells, he had quite a reputation. Now yes, I did have a fun summer of showing my ass, however, round the way boys were off-limits. I didn't sleep with the homies. I only had fun with guys from other neighborhoods, so I could always keep my respect in my hood. He called again two days later from another phone number.

"Yo! What the fuck? Why you ain't answer your phone?" he yelled.

"My bad. I got caught up. What's up?" I asked in an apologetic tone.

"Oh, you play a lot of games. You were caught up, huh?" he asked with aggression.

"I apologize. I didn't mean to stand you up," I lied.

"Well, I'm still trying to go out. So, What's up?"

"Wow, you are persistent, huh? Well, I come as a team. I have a son; you will have to take him out too."

"That's definitely cool. Where you want to go?" Kells asked.

"We can go somewhere simple like Applebees. My son loves french fries," I giggled.

"Applebees it is. I can't wait to see you. Don't be bluffing this time either," he said with force.

"I won't. It's a date. See you then."

Kells aggressive personality piqued my interest. Kells took Zi and I on a date to Applebees. Zi was two years old and the coolest kid ever. He never cried, complained, or had any issues. He just wanted to giggle and eat. He was mellow, and he listened well. He looked just like me, and in my eyes, he was the perfect kid. When we arrived, Kells took Zi out his seatbelt and carried the entire car seat inside the restaurant. I was impressed that he got my son first, and I walked behind them. From the moment we sat down, we laughed, joked, and played the entire date. He was nothing like the image I had of him. He had swag and more personality I gave him credit for. Zi was down to his last fries, and I could tell he was full because he sucked the fries to mush instead of chewing them.

"You almost ready? I didn't really like my food," I complained while looking at my full plate of food.

"Yeah, me either. Shit was nasty for real," Kells agreed.

"You sure did eat it, though," I laughed.

"I can't deny that. So, when can we hang out again?" he quizzed.

"I actually had fun with you. We can definitely hang out again. We shouldn't even pay for this nasty ass food," I joked.

"Yup, fuck it! It was nasty, anyway. I will stop and get you something to eat from somewhere else," Kells said as he snapped Zi in his car seat.

"I was just joking about not paying the bill," I confessed.

"I wasn't! The boy and I are out," he said as he grabbed the car seat and the baby bag and walked towards the restaurant entrance.

"Oh, my goodness. You are crazy," I whispered as I hurried to catch up with them.

Soon as we made it to the front door, we ran. The sight of seeing Kells run with a car seat and a baby bag was hilarious, and I couldn't stop laughing. Our first date was an adventure. Zi and I went back to Kells's apartment in Downtown Baltimore instead of going home. Kells and I both wanted our date to continue. His apartment was small and cozy, like a bachelor's pad. He put on the Disney movie "Madagascar" for Zi to watch, but we both enjoyed watching the movie as well. I found myself laughing at the little adult humor they slid in the film. It didn't take long before Zi was knocked out snoring. I walked over to my son and kissed all over his chubby cheeks. I admired his precious face and the drool leaking from his lips. I took off his shoes and smelled his feet, I frowned my face at his stinky feet. I could feel Kells watching my every move. I could feel his eyes glaring at me. I refused to acknowledge the stares. I wondered would he look away, but he didn't. I was flattered at the thought of how much he seemed to like me.

I laid next to Kells on his bed. I had no intention of having sex with him, especially not on the first date. It had been a while since I had sex. I wasn't seriously dating anyone at the time. Kells kissed my neck, and I turned away. He kissed my neck again, and I let him. I decided not to show any of my kinkiness. I figured since he liked me so much, I should let him devour my body. I should let him take in my scent and please my body's desires. He claimed to have wanted me so bad, so that was his opportunity to show it. I let my body relax into the bed. I let go of all tension and let him take control.

He softly kissed every inch of my body as though he had been waiting for the moment to meet my skin against his lips. He kissed my thighs, and instead of making his way to my girl, he kissed further down. I thought, *why is he kissing down there? He can come back up to my vagina. What the fuck is happening? Maybe I should grab his head and pull him back up to my girl. Wow that feels amazing. Maybe he was on to something going down there. Relax Sunni.* My mind was racing. He snatched me out of my thoughts when I felt the warmest sensation hovered around my toes. His fourplay immediately sent a signal to my clitoris, which was pumping out of control. The feeling was unbelievable. He looked up at me and noticed my body moving around with anticipation.

He made his way back up to my girl and finished her off in a matter of seconds. My legs trembled with anxiety as I waited for him to put on the condom. My body was hot and ready for him to enter. He slowly entered my world and slowly stroked. He pounded with rhythm and consistency. He fucked me like he wanted me to know that his pipe had been waiting to meet my walls. The introduction was explosive. He picked me up off the bed and held me up against the wall and deep stroked me while holding me in the air. He was showing off and giving it to me, so I would be sure to come back for more. After we both released, we laid there in a spoon position and fell asleep.

That was it! He caught me up, and I was at his place every day. That fast, we were rocking together, and we wasted no time committing to each other. I completely disregarded all the warning signs. Zi and I stayed at his place 3 times a week, and he stayed at my place on the remaining days. I was feeling him, and the feeling was mutual. I was at his apartment one day when he stopped home for a quickie. The entire time we were having sex, his phone kept ringing.

"Who keeps calling your phone like that?" I questioned Kells as we were having sex.

"Fuck that phone!" he quickly replied.

"That shit getting on my nerves. Answer it or cut it off or something," I said as I hopped off his penis. Kells phone annoyed me, and I didn't know why it was getting under my skin. He cursed and walked over to his phone. I glanced to see who was calling.

"That's just Little Destiny from around the way. She probably needs me to bring more stuff when I come back outside."

"So why you didn't answer? Why would someone be so pressed to hang up and call back a hundred times?"

"Why are you asking me? I don't know Sunni, she's young. Bring your ass back over here," Kells demanded.

"No, thanks. I'm out of the mood. Go ahead back outside. I'm a stay at my house tonight," I said as I snapped my bra back on.

"You serious? You really acting like that because my phone was ringing? That's cute. My baby jealous," Kells said with a smirk.

"I'm not jealous, nor am I stupid. Something doesn't seem right, and that's not the first time she blew your phone up like that."

"Would you feel better if I called her. Damn! I can't believe you tripping."

"Nope. You don't have to call her. You said it's nothing than it's nothing, but I will approach her when I see her and ask for myself."

Kells left out angry. This was our first fight but wouldn't be our last. I asked people around the way what was the deal with them two. I was told they use to talk. I was a little shocked to hear that because she was so young. Destiny was a cute, young, dark brown-skinned slim girl from around the way. She hung out with the homies, and according to the streets, Kells was her first.

Kells and I were getting closer and closer, and the phone calls stopped, or he put his phone on mute when I was around. We decided that he would move in with Zi and I and let his apartment go. It didn't make sense to keep paying bills at both places, and we were together every night. Before the decision was final, I decided to make sure nothing was really going on with Destiny and Kells, so I took a ride around the way and pulled up on Oliver Street. I saw Destiny standing on one side of the street and Kells on the other. I decided not to acknowledge him, and I walked straight up to Destiny.

"Hey, Destiny. Can I talk to you for a second?" I asked as I walked up on her and a few other people we both knew.

"Yeah, what's up?" she asked in a nonchalant tone.

"Kells and I are official now. He's about to move in with me. Before I get too deep with him, I just wanted to know do y'all have something going on?"

"Did you ask him that?" she questioned with a smirk.

"I did ask him. He said it's nothing! So, I'm just asking you! Men lie, and I'm not about to be playing with my feelings."

"If he said it ain't nothing than it ain't nothing. Everything is good," Destiny said as she looked in Kells direction.

I walked over to Kells, who had a look of concern. He stared at us the entire time we talked. He pretended he was unbothered, but I could tell his balls were sweating from fear. The curiosity was killing him, and he couldn't wait to question me.

"What was that about?" Kells asked soon as I crossed the street.

"Why? And why the fuck do you look scared?" I questioned.

"I ain't got shit to be scared about. Everybody knows you are my wife," he said as he glanced over to Destiny.

"Yeah, ok. See you later," I said as I started to walk to the car.

"See me later? Wait, you leaving without giving me a kiss or nothing? We good, right? Come here," he demanded.

"Yeah, we good," I said as I walked over and wrapped my arms around Kells, and tongue kissed him.

"You know I love you, right?" he asked, staring in my eyes.

"Yeah Kells, I know. You know I will kill you, right?" I asked in a serious face.

"Yeah Sunni, I know."

Kells moved in that weekend. Marco and I co-parenting relationship got complicated. He didn't agree with me dating Kells at all. Marco was sure to voice his opinion every chance he got. Marco worked a lot, and he spent time with Zi whenever it was convenient. He didn't have a set schedule with him. Sometimes months would pass by since he last saw him, but he frequently called to check on him. Marco did all the responsible parent duties. He paid for Zi health insurance, made sure he had a life policy, made sure he had active dental coverage and that type of stuff. Marco called me one day extremely upset. I answered the phone with one hand and a bar of soap in the other.

"Sunni! Have you lost your fucking mind? What's wrong with you?" Marco screamed.

"Marco, what are you talking about? I'm getting Zi out the tub, can I call you back?" I asked as I wrapped the towel around Zi's naked body and picked him up.

"No, you can't call me back. You got my son calling Yo daddy now?"

"Marco, Zi know who his father is. I told him to stop calling him that, but he is with him every day, and he really doesn't understand," I calmly explained.

"I'm not trying to hear that shit! Why is he with him every day anyway? What are you doing? Do you know who you are fucking with?"

"Here we go again. Please let's not do the "Kells" thing again. That's my boyfriend whether you like it or not. I'm tired of talking about this with you."

"No, I'm a keep trying to talk some sense into your ass. He's a fucking whore. You deserve better. You are being stupid and naïve. I know exactly who he is!" Marco yelled while breathing heavily.

"I know who he is too. Far as our son goes, maybe you should spend more time with him, and he won't be so confused. Don't blame all this on me. I never pressure you or ask you for shit! I knew what it was when I decided to have him, so I don't bother you, Marco. I let you play whatever role you want."

"So, you calling me a bad father now. I fucking hate you, Yo. You are going to regret fucking with that freak ball ass boyfriend of yours!" Marco hollered.

"I never said you were a bad father. Did you just say you hate me?" I questioned in a low tone.

"Yup, I hate you now!" Marco said as he slammed the phone down in my ear.

A sadness instantly came over me. Marco was my friend, and he never said he hated me before. We had arguments and sometimes physical fights, but we never said strong words like "hate." Actually, we always apologized and made up after our disagreements. This time was different. Marco stopped calling me to check on Zi; instead, he started getting his mother to do everything. She started calling me to pick him up, or just to check on Zi. Marco and I relationship died that day. We didn't even speak when we saw each other. It killed me to lose my friend, but we were both too stubborn to make it right.

Kells and I got baby fever. We started planning for us to get pregnant. We both wanted a girl. We had sex multiple times a day, and I wore his ass out. He would complain that I was killing him. I laughed and raped him whenever I felt like it. With all the sex we had, it didn't take long before I was pregnant. Everything was going good until this one day, I got a call from my friend who informed me Kells was on Patterson Park hugged up with Destiny. My heart broke in a million pieces. I called him and told him to come home right away. I pretended something was wrong with my pregnancy. Kells rushed home, and I wasted no time grilling him when he walked through the door.

"So, you hugged up with Bitches in public now?" I screamed in his face soon as he walked through the door.

"What the fuck are you talking about?" Kells asked with a confused face.

"Don't play dumb. You were outside hugged up on Destiny. I'm so fucking stupid," I yelled as tears slowly ran down my cheeks.

"Don't cry. Sunni, I wasn't hugged up with no one. Come on, use your brain that doesn't even make sense."

"No, you should've used your brain and had more respect for me. You killed my trust. I'm sitting here carrying your child, and your disrespectful ass hugged up with Bitches in broad daylight," I cried.

"How stupid do you think I am? Why the fuck would I do that? That's dumb. You are emotional. Come here," he said as he put his arm out to hug me.

"I'm not emotional and get your dirty ass arms away from me. You look dirty to me now!" I screamed.

"This shit is dumb. I'm not even going to argue with you!" Kells yelled with aggression.

I went into the bedroom and laid on the bed and slumped into the pillows and cried my eyes out. I squeezed the other pillows tight and hugged them as if they were my baby. I so badly wished Zi was home, but he was at my sister Honey's house for the weekend. Hugging Zi always made me feel better. Kells walked into the room and laid behind me and put his arms around me. I moved his arms, and he put them back around me tighter. I was too weak to move them again. I was hurt, and the pain was burning a hole in my heart. He held me while I cried. He occasionally whispered, "I didn't do anything, please stop crying. I would never hurt you."

I cried myself to sleep. I woke up the next morning with Kells heavy arm still around me. He laid there peacefully snoring. I took his arm from around my waist and threw it off of me. We had both fell asleep in street clothes. We never laid in our bed with outside clothes, and I felt so dirty. I felt dirty from the clothes and dirty from him. I went to take a shower. I stepped in the hot shower, and I felt numb. I cried and talked to myself. *How could I be so stupid? He has been fucking with her all along. All those months. I hope they used protection. He's a fucking liar. I hate him. I fucking asked her were they dealing with each other. Now my dumb ass is pregnant. Marco said he would hurt me, he fucking told me. I'm so stupid.* My thoughts were interrupted by a knock on the bathroom door.

"What?" I screamed from the shower.

"Can I come in?" Kells yelled through the door.

"Fuck no! You need to go!" I yelled.

"I'm not going anywhere. This my family! You are overreacting. I told you nothing happened. I'm a smack the shit out of your friend for lying too. I think I know who it was," he said as he stepped in the shower.

"You better not put your hands on none of my friends cause you a damn dog. Here, you can have the shower. I'm getting out."

"No, you not," he said as he grabbed my belly. He softly rolled his hands around my stomach in circles.

"Get your dirty hands off of us. Oh, and I need my car. I'm not sitting in this house anymore. Pregnant or not. Fuck this relationship!"

I stepped out of the shower and got dressed. I drove to West Baltimore to meet up with my friends. I didn't want to chance bumping into him on Oliver street. I decided to start going outside, although I couldn't smoke, drink, or party. I could still watch everyone else have fun. My friends were the best, and they really spoiled me when I was pregnant. They fed me before the kids, they carried stuff for me and gave me whatever I wanted. I really loved them.

When Kells pissed me off, I starved him. I wouldn't cook for weeks at a time. I also wouldn't talk to him for weeks. The house had a cold vibe after he was exposed. I tried to stay out of the house as much as possible. I went to Oliver Street one day with Missy. We bumped into Marco's cousin Tesa who I use to hang out with on Curley Street. Well, now Tesa was Zi, cousin, too, since I had a baby by Marco. To my surprise, Tesa was also pregnant. We couldn't go inside the bar with pregnant bellies because our friends would curse us out. We just decided to hang outside of the bar since we were both pregnant. We comfortably sat on butt cushions to avoid the pain of the hard-concrete steps.

"My doctor said I can have one big glass of wine a day. What are you trying to do?" I asked Tesa.

"My doctor said the same damn thing. I think we should get us some wine," Tesa replied.

"Missy, can you get us some wine out the bar?" I asked nicely.

"Hell no! Y'all fat asses are plotting. My doctor never told me I could have no damn wine. Y'all not messing my nieces up," Missy fussed and laughed.

"Shut up and get the damn wine," Tesa barked in a joking way.

"Nieces? You are having a girl too, Tesa?" I asked.

"Yup, I'm having a girl too. That's crazy. Missy here's the money," Tesa said as she shoved the money in Missy direction.

"I never thought you would have kids," I admitted to Tesa.

"I know, right. Sometimes I can't believe it myself," Tesa said as she rubbed her belly.

Missy purchased us a bottle of Moscato. We sat on the steps and drunk the entire bottle together. We talked about pregnant issues and how we both were obsessed with watching "A Baby Story" on the network TLC. Something about watching a woman in labor was obsessive when I was pregnant. I did the same thing when I was pregnant with Zi. I always stopped watching after I gave birth. We laughed and talked for hours. We even snuck around the corner to get another bottle of wine to share. I told Tesa, "It's only crushed grapes, we'll be fine." Tesa's baby was jumping around like crazy in her belly. She grabbed my hand and put it on her stomach, and I laughed at how energetic her baby was. What I didn't know at the time was the baby I was touching in Tesa's stomach was the child of one of my children's father. I will let you decide which one! Nothing is ever what it seems. Come on, flip the page…

CHAPTER 6

FIRST NIGHT OUT

The next few months of pregnancy were a drag. I was so emotional, and the little girl I carried in my belly was turning me into a cry baby. I cried for everything. My hormones were out of control, and I drove myself crazy. Kells and I eventually worked through our issues with the "Destiny situation." I told myself if anything ever came up about her again, I would leave him on the spot. It didn't matter if I was pregnant or if I had to raise two kids alone. I wasn't putting up with a cheating man. Kells never missed one doctor visit, and he was obsessively in love with our unborn child. He talked to my belly all the time, and he claimed that she would look just like him. We argued over her name for months, and I eventually let him name her because I was tired of fighting.

My ankles were so swollen at the end of my pregnancy, and the doctor told me I had to take it easy. I was tired of being pregnant. Unlike my first pregnancy, I wasn't working at my job as much towards the end, which caused me to get extremely bored. I drove Kells crazy too. He had to bring me watermelon every day from one specific stall in Northeast Market. If he tried to bring it from somewhere else, I always knew, and I would immediately start crying. I had never been so emotional in my life. I had officially offered my daughter an eviction notice. Since Zi was a big baby in size at the time of his birth, I shamefully lied to my doctor and told her I had to get induced to avoid complications. She put a long needle in my stomach to ensure the baby's lungs were healthy enough to induce me and bam I was having my baby. At 37 weeks, I had a beautiful 7oz baby girl that looked exactly like Kells. We named her Tira.

After giving birth to Tira, I was a complete disaster. I went through postpartum depression again. I felt fat and unattractive. Kells was kind, and he always reminded me I was beautiful. The depression didn't last as long as the first time I went through postpartum depression. I was walking around the house, nagging, and complaining. I hadn't been out for the first two months after having Tira. I only went to the market or the clinic for follow-ups.

"Why you keep nagging? You are getting on me and the kid's nerves," Kells said as he kissed all over Tira's face.

"Cause I'm tired of doing everything in here," I said as I angrily picked up a toy off the floor.

"Do what Sunni? I wash all the clothes. You just cook, clean, and lately bitch."

"Are you crazy? That's all I do? I boil bottles, and I'm the one who gets up in the middle of the night and I..." I started to continue my rant when Kells cut me off.

"Okay, you do a lot, damn. Go outside. Go, have some fun, I'll keep the kids. You are being a pain in our ass. Right, little mama?" he asked Tira and smiled at Zi.

"I don't even have anything to wear. I wasn't this size before I got pregnant. You know what? I am complaining. I'll find something to wear and get the hell out of here."

"Thank you! Have fun!" Kells sarcastically responded.

I took a shower and got dressed to go outside. I found a brand new BeBe shirt that I had mistakenly bought too big before I got pregnant. I was able to squeeze in a pair of jeans that I had way in the back of my closet. I put on some mascara, kiss the family, and hit the streets. As I prepared to go outside, I had no idea how this night would change my life forever. I had no idea I would never forget the outfit I wore. Every little detail of this day would forever be a memory in my mind. I knew my first stop was going to be at Sherry's Bar, and then I would decide my next move once I saw who was outside. I was hoping to see Licia and Missy.

I went to the girl Mya's house. Mya lived on the same street as Sherry's bar. She lived on the other end of the street, but you could see the bar from her house. I parked my car in front of Mya's house and knocked on her door before I walked up to Sherry's bar. Of course, she answered with a blunt ready to smoke. Mya was a cute chocolate girl that was a mutual friend of mine and Kells. She was closer to Kells, but she liked me too. Zi looked at her like an aunt, so I always adored their relationship. We smoked and decided to walk up to Sherry's to have a drink. It was a lot of people outside. Everyone was smoking and drinking. The bar was crowded, as a beautiful Friday night would be. Ms. Sherry had just cracked down on the new law that forbids smoking in the bars. Initially, she ignored it and still allowed people to smoke cigarettes, but she had finally started cracking down. So, more people were outside, much more than usual, because they wanted to drink and smoke simultaneously.

To me, this was an ordinary live day in the hood until it was not so ordinary. I was inside the bar laughing and talking trash to everyone. I got many compliments on how good I looked with some weight on me. That made me feel good. I looked up, and I saw Marco. I was shocked to see Marco. He didn't hang out, and he wasn't the bar hopping type. He played chess and spades with the old heads on Chester Street. My heart started beating fast when I saw him. We hadn't talked in months, and we never got cool after that day he told me, he hates me and hung up on me. He walked right up to me.

"What's up, Trouble?" Marco asked in a friendly tone.

"Hey, Nasty Marco!" I laughed. It was funny we called each other old nicknames. I was relieved he was in a good mood.

"Congratulations on the baby. You had a girl, right?"

"Yup, she's a girl. Thank you. What are you doing here?" I questioned.

"It's my birthday! I just came around to get a drink before I make my way up to Chester Street."

"What's today? Oh, it is your birthday. Happy birthday Baby Daddy!" I said with excitement.

"Thanks. Let me buy you a drink. Sit down and have a drink with me for my birthday," Marco asked with a big smile on his face.

"I can't let you buy the drinks. It's your birthday. I got you. Tell Ms. Sherry what you want."

"Well, I'm glad I bumped into you. I really miss our friendship. We had a lot of fun together, and you always kept me laughing," Marco confessed.

"I missed you too, Marco. I wanted to end this war a long time ago, but I was too stubborn," I admitted.

"Yeah, I was angry too. I always loved you, and I just wanted better for you. If you weren't going to be with me, I wanted you with a good man. I still handled the situation all wrong."

"Shit, me too. I understood where you were coming from about Zi calling another man Daddy. You had the right to be frustrated," I said as I look towards the door to see who entered the bar.

"I never want to lose our friendship again. I'm going to do better with my son too. He is an amazing little boy. He couldn't be more perfect. Can I get him tomorrow?" he asked.

"You know you can. I understand now that you were looking out for me with Kells. I won't sit here, and bad talk him because I love him, but I will admit you were right," I said as I took another sip from my cup.

"I won't say I told you so. I'll just leave that alone," Marco said as he glanced around the room.

"Yup, let's just leave that alone," I agreed.

"You should give me some birthday pussy. I turned 40 today. I deserve some of that," Marco licked his lips as his eyes were locked on my vagina.

"You better stop playing Nasty Marco. You know, once I give you a taste of this, you will be right back on my heels. Go ahead and order another drink for us. I'm a put some more money in the jukebox," I laughed and got up and walked away.

Marco and I sat and talked for about an hour. He told me he had a little friend he was digging. I caught him up with everything that had been going on in my life. We drank and laughed like we were the only two in the bar. It wasn't long before the counter was full of empty shot glasses. Of course, he flirted, and I flirted back, but nothing substantial. I had almost forgotten I was with Mya. I lost track of the time while talking with Marco. I wanted to get some air and see what kind of action was happening outside of the bar. Before I got up, Marco asked for a hug. I gave him the fakest hug ever. The more he squeezed, the less I squeezed. He held me so tight for some reason. Like really tight, and it made me feel weird. Just Marco and I standing in the middle of the lounge, hugging tightly, was not the image I wanted people to see. I was afraid people would run to Kells and say, "Sunni was hugged up in the bar with Marco." That was an issue I wanted to avoid at all costs. So, I barely hugged him.

We got outside, and everyone was hanging out, all my homeboys and all my homegirls. I saw Licia, but she already had plans to go to a club downtown, and I didn't want to leave the block. We stood around, smoking, and joking with each other. Marco probably was the only working man out there. Mostly everyone else was drug dealers or killers. Marco stood there, smoking a blunt when I walked over to him.

"I thought you were leaving?" I asked.

"I am about to leave. I just wanted to smoke real quick. Why? You trying to leave with me?" Marco asked with lustering eyes.

"You never quit, huh? Let me hit that blunt," I asked.

"You know I will always try. Here, Trouble," Marco said as he handed me an unlit blunt.

"You let the fire go out. Give me a light."

"Damn, you want me to smoke it for you too?" he asked in a sarcastic tone.

"Don't be smart. Have fun around the corner, acting like an old man. Enjoy your birthday Marco!" I said in an excited tone as I handed him back the blunt.

"Okay, I'll see you tomorrow when I get my son. I love you, Trouble," he blurted out.

"Love you too, Marco," I whispered before I walked away towards Mya.

"Sunni let's go down my house," Mya suggested.

"Why, girl? It's live out here. We can have fun out here for real!" I said with excitement.

"Look around. It's too many people out here. Let's just take a walk down to the house," she said as she grabbed my arm and attached it to hers.

We got to the end of the block and we heard massive gunshots. It sounded like a war in Iraq. It resembled machine guns, and it was more shots fired than usual. My heart raced with anxiety. Mya looked at me with big eyes, and we ran across the street to get to her house. We ran in the house, and before she could lock the door, a few other people we knew were running towards her house, so we quickly let them in and locked the door. The room was silent as we heard nothing but gunshots—***Pop Pop Pop Pop Pop***. No one talked. Every pop I heard; I slowly blinked my eyes. We stared at each other with intensity. I held my breath until I listened to the last gunshot. We all stood in silence.

"I fucking hate this city, we can never just have fun," I said in a sad voice.

"Damn, that was a lot of fucking shots," Mya said.

"I know. That shit was so painful to hear. I'm going the fuck home with my family," I said in a disgusted tone.

"Wait, you can't go home. We have to walk up there. All our friends up there, Sunni," Mya said with a look of concern.

"Fuck! I'm so upset. I didn't even think about all our friends. Shit, Mike, and them up there too. Yeah, we have to walk up there. Let me just sit down real quick," I said in a scared tone. My anxiety was getting the best of me.

"We don't have time for you to sit down. They might need us. We don't know who got shot. Come on!" Mya demanded.

Soon as we opened the front door, we heard yelling and chaos. People were screaming excruciating screams. It was the sound of terror. We gained the courage to walk towards Sherry's bar. It was like a bloody scene from a movie. Every step I took, I felt like I was in a dream, well more like a nightmare. We saw people shot in different places. Some of my friends were shot. A few of them were shot in the leg or the arms, some people were shot in more severe areas. We told them to apply pressure, as we had seen in the movies. Mya and I ran from person to person trying to help. The entire block was filled with people running around screaming.

I saw Tesa's and Marco's Aunt Roxy on the ground on her knees with a crowd around her. I couldn't tell if she was shot from where I stood. I continued to help people as I tried to make my way to Roxy. For some reason, my feet felt stuck like I was in quicksand. Every step was a hard step to take. I was traumatized and emotionally drained. Mya walked ahead of me to get to where Roxy was. I finally got closer, and Mya blocked my way.

"Come on, Sunni. Let's go back that way. Let's make sure Mike is okay," Mya said in a weak voice.

"What's up with Aunt Roxy? Is she shot?" I asked in a concerned tone.

"She good. Come on, please," Mya begged with a fragile voice.

"No! I want to make sure she's good. Why would a crowd be around her?" I quizzed as I pushed past Mya.

I walked up and instantly recognized the outfit of the person lying in the gutter. I fell to my knees in agony. My heart pumped out my chest, and I shook uncontrollably.

"Oh, my God! Marco no! Please Nooooo! Get the fuck up! Get up, Marco!" I screamed and cried.

"Hold on, Marco. The ambulance is coming. Hold on. Stay with me," Aunt Roxy pleaded in a soft tone. She was on her knees over top of Marco's head, rocking slowly.

"Someone call the ambulance. What the fuck is taking so long!" Mya blurted out.

"Marco, I love you. I love you. Come on. Please fight. You have to get Zi tomorrow, remember?" I said as I squeezed Marco's hand as salty tears and drool filled my face.

"Hmmm, Hmm, Zi," Marco tried to speak, but nothing but faint sounds and blood came out of his mouth.

"Don't talk! Just hold on Marco, they coming," Roxy said again as she rocked back and forth.

"Marco, I'm sorry for everything. You are going to be okay. You have to be okay. Where is he shot? I don't even see no wounds or blood. Fight for your kids, Marco. You must fight, you hear me? Don't give up," I said as I looked in Marco's eyes, which were now rolling around uncontrollably.

Marco lost his grip on my hand, he was no longer squeezing tight like before, and his hand slowly let go of mines. I felt death take him. I felt his soul leave his body. I saw his spirit leave his eyes, and his eyes now stared sharply with no emotion. I felt him give up the fight, and he died right there in front of me. I laid in his chest and screamed. I'm not quite sure how I got off him, but I remember someone picking me up. The next few moments were a blur. I screamed in agony, and when I came back to reality, I was back in front of Mya's house. I looked up the street and saw Marco's stiff body lying there all alone.

They put yellow tape around him, threw a white cloth over him, and left him on the ground like a dead dog. I wanted to lay in the gutter with him until he got to the morgue. I wanted him to know he wasn't alone. To say I was devastated would be a severe understatement. I was numb. I was in disbelief, and I was in more pain than I had ever encountered my entire life. I stared at his body on the ground as tears streamed down my face. I had flashbacks of the entire conversation we just had in the bar. I thought of the first time I met him and how I bit his bottom lip. I thought about all the nights we wrestled around the house naked. I thought about the day he held Zi in his arms and said, "He's beautiful. Thank you for keeping him Sunni." Then I thought of my son, my now fatherless son, and I screamed a painful cry. Everyone tried to console me. I stood there and mumbled nonsense. My mind had gone through a brief moment of insanity. Every conversation, every time we fucked, every time he picked up Zi, every argument, every fun moment, every phone call, every time he smiled, it all came crashing down on me. I glanced back up the street, and there he still laid lifeless, breathless, and deceased.

I couldn't bear to look at him any longer, so I slowly walked to my car and opened the door. I intended to pull right off, but I couldn't move. I banged the steering wheel repeatedly screaming, "FUCK FUCK FUCK!" I was pissed with God, the Killer, the Devil, and everyone else. I had questions for God. *Why did I have to be there? Why did he die? Why not one of the murdering Bitches that deserved it? Why on his birthday? Why my son's father? Why does my son have to grow up without a father? Why the working man? Why didn't I hug him tight? Why? Why? Why?*

"The hug," would haunt me for years. It was my biggest regret from that night. I cared what people would think, and I missed the opportunity to show him true love. I missed the privilege of squeezing him tight and indulging in his scent just one more time. I gave him a fake hug, and that was weak and fraudulent. When he hugged me so tight in the bar, I wanted to breathe slowly in his arms and squeeze him back. I desired to lay on his chest and feel his heartbeat as I inhaled his presence. That's what I really wanted. Instead of doing what I wanted to do, I cared more about what people who meant nothing to me would think. I felt a slight moment of happiness to know we made up that night. That felt good. He didn't die upset with me, and that cleared my conscious. It's the very reason I don't hold grudges to this day.

I called Kells and just cried the entire ride home. He didn't say one word; he just listened to me cry. I managed to get back home without jumping off a bridge from temporary insanity. I ran to Kells and hugged him, and he gave me the same fake hug I gave Marco earlier that day. I lost something for Kells that night. He seemed jealous and unsympathetic. He appeared agitated as if I were crying too much for an ex-boyfriend. He didn't consider the fact that I saw Marco's body lose life or that he was my son's father. He wanted me to get over it and fast. I couldn't. I was hurt. Zi was three years old when his father was accidentally murdered in the streets. The bullets Marco took was for the guy

120

who stood next to him. He was literally at the wrong place at the wrong time. My first night out turned into a deadly night. The Baltimore Sun newspaper read, "9 shot and one fatality." Marco's birth date was also his death date, and it was also the day I officially became A DAMAGED woman.

CHAPTER 7

WHITE PRIVILEGE OR UNEDUCATED?

White Privilege: is the societal privilege that benefits white people over non-white people, particularly if they are otherwise under the same social, political, or economic circumstances.

Uneducated: lacking an education; poorly educated.

Things had drastically changed after Marco's death. I tried to grieve fast and move on. I didn't want death to consume me once again. There were two issues with trying to avoid grief, I had a piece of

Marco left behind (my son), and I saw Marco take his last breath. Both issues traumatized me. Rushing the grieving process would not be easy. If you don't go through the tough parts of life and try to avoid them instead of feeling them, you will hold on to a lot of pain and baggage. I avoided what happened, and I blocked out the existence of Marco all together. My mind wouldn't allow me to think of him the way I did prior to his death. All my mind could see was his last moments of life, which constantly kept me in a state of shock and instant depression.

A couple of months went by, and Kells and I struggled to keep our relationship together. He was showing his ass, and I was always stuck in the house with the baby. When I only had one child, I still had freedom. Anyone would watch Zi for me. He was a good boy; he could walk, talk, use the bathroom on his own, and he never caused a fuss. It's not so easy getting a sitter for a newborn. I felt stuck and overwhelmed. I loved being a mother to both of my kids, but I lost, "ME" in the process.

Sometimes as parents, we indulge in our kid's happiness so much that we forget to take care of ourselves. We forget that we are people, too, with wants and desires. Kells felt he was fair by giving me a break because he still took Zi with him on most days. It wasn't really a break for me because I still had the baby. This was the day Kells lost his damn mind. It was also the day our relationship would spiral downhill from a reckless decision he decided to make. It was 3:00 in the morning on a Thursday night, and Kells was not home yet. I started calling his phone and got no answer. I instantly worried something happened to him because, sadly, living in Baltimore, a bad thought is always the first thought. I called all the hospitals and the police station. I called Kells repeatedly. Around 5:00 in the morning, I got a call from his phone number.

"Hello. Kells?" I asked in a half-sleep voice.

"Hey, Sunni. This is Mike. Kells is at my house sleep on the sofa," Mike said in an explanatory tone.

"What? What the fuck is he doing sleep at your house?" I questioned with authority.

"Sis, calm down. You know this man doesn't drink, and he decided to get drunk. He couldn't handle his liquor, and we threw his ass on the couch," Mike explained.

"Really, Mike? Come on now. You expect me to believe that bullshit?" I asked with anger.

"It's the truth. I didn't want you to be worried with the kids, so I called you from his phone," he explained in a convincing tone.

"Oh, I must have stupid written on my forehead. Kells is a fucking coward to get you to call. Put him on the phone!" I demanded.

"He's sleep. We've been trying to get him up for the last hour."

"Where is the car?" I asked feeling defeated.

"It's here. Everything good, Sis," Mike said calmly.

"Tell that Bitch, if he don't get his ass in this house within the next hour, he won't have a house to come to!" I yelled.

I hung up the phone, and I immediately felt many emotions. I felt relieved Kells wasn't dead or in jail than I instantly felt angry that he stayed out all night. His disrespect had reached a new level. He had never stayed out all night, and I felt insulted that he thought I would believe his bullshit drunk story. I felt he needed to pay, but I had to go to work in a few hours, and he had to help me get the kids settled. He made it in the house an hour later, making noises as if his stomach was in excruciating pain. He whined and complained of a headache. He went all out on the drunk man scam. I paid his ass no mind, and I talked myself into not smacking him for disrespecting our relationship. Kells thought because we had a brand-new baby, I would put up with his crap. He would soon see that he had the wrong one. It wasn't time to show him how wrong he was, just yet.

When a woman gets quiet, a man better pay attention. He shouldn't take her silence lightly. Instead of hitting him upside his head with a hammer, I remained silent. I pretended he didn't stay out all night. I didn't have the energy to argue with him or hear his lies. The damage was done. He had lost my respect. No talking, fussing, or fighting was going to fix that. In my mind, whoever he was with, he liked her so much that he risked his family. That was all I needed to know to decide to give up on us. I let him rest peacefully like the fake, sick, hungover liar he was.

I got dressed and went to work. My energy was off, and I felt horrible on the inside. I had been up all night worrying and crying. I couldn't hide the fact that something was wrong because my eyes were puffy and red. My co-workers were concerned, and they whispered around the office to see if someone knew what happened to me. I kind of wanted to shut up the whispers and say, "Hey, everyone! I have an announcement! Last night my boyfriend stuck his hard-hot dick in someone's vagina. Now, can you please stop whispering?" Instead, I just sat at my desk with a broken heart. I just wished for the workday to be over with no more issues. Tasha walked over to my desk with a young white female that I had never seen around the office before.

"Hey, Sunni. You okay?" Tasha asked with a concerned look on her face.

"Yeah, I'm good, Tasha. What can I do for you? I will give you my final billing report at the end of the day," I said as I looked at the timid young girl who stood behind her.

"Oh, no rush for the billing report. I actually came over to introduce you to Sandy. She is our new biller."

"Hi, Sandy. Nice to meet you. Welcome to the team!" I said to Sandy in a weak but friendly voice.

"Nice to meet you too, Sunni. I'm excited to be working with you. They say you are the best. Hopefully, you will be patient with me," Sandy said with a smile.

"Patient with you?" I asked in a confused tone.

"Yes, Sunni. That's why we came over because we need you to train Sandy. We told her you know everything, and she'll be in good hands with you. We know you will be a great asset to Sandy."

I was the top biller for a promotion company called Webb's that I worked for in Hunt Valley. I started the job when I was in high school as a temp in the warehouse. I soon became the warehouse supervisor; from there, I went to the office as an Accounts Receivable biller; lastly, I was a trainer in the billing department. Tasha and I became cool again after the little marriage argument we had years ago when I was dating Marco. Although we let the topic go, our friendship was never the same. I thought she was too judgmental, and she thought I was a backstabbing husband thief. We just stop discussing our personal life altogether. To me, this training would be no different from any other training that I provided a new biller. I soon realized this young lady would change everything in my life.

Over the years, while working at Webb's, I caused a lot of chaos. I vocally spoke up about how I felt anytime I wanted to, which caused me to get far in the company. I received mixed feelings from my black co-workers. Some of them envied me because they felt the big bosses favored me, but they had it wrong. I was genuinely a hard worker, and I didn't bite my tongue. I asked for raises, and I spoke up when I felt I was mistreated. I also applied for positions I had no experience in because I was confident that I could learn any role in the company. I loved a challenge. I took on a considerable challenge a few years prior when I worked in the warehouse and gave this speech to my fellow co-workers as I stood on a chair in the cold warehouse.

"Why are we here? Did we not give up enough as people for the right to be off on this day like everyone else? Don't we deserve to be a part of the mighty dream Dr. Martin Luther King had for us? Is the post office closed? Are the banks closed? Weren't we just off for that Jewish holiday? Don't we deserve to be at the MLK parade? I say we stand up and all be sick and get the fuck out of here to make a statement. We want this day off like everyone else. I feel a headache coming on. Who is with me?"

I jumped down from my chair after I finished my rant and walked to grab my coat. I made a statement, and my co-workers agreed. I repeatedly asked the company why did we have to work on MLK day? They told me they didn't recognize it as a national holiday, even though their warehouse workers were pretty much all Black. Well, that year, I was tired, and I stood up and spoke up. We all said we were sick and left except two girls who feared losing their job. They couldn't fire all of us. As a team, we stood firm. All my co-workers and I got in our cars and rode to the MLK parade and celebrated his life and dreams like everyone else. These strong stand up moments in my life was not a big deal to me at the time. I had a strong influence on people and had no idea how to use it. Well, training Sandy would be another stand-up moment for me; I just didn't know it at the time. The next morning, I rolled my chair to Sandy cubicle and sat next to her desk.

"You ready to train?" I asked Sandy with excitement.

"Yup! Please don't get frustrated. I hardly know anything about computers," Sandy said in a low tone so the other employees wouldn't hear her.

"Do you know how to use the number keys? That's important in billing. We bill fast here."

"No. I will learn, though."

"Yup, just practice at home. How did you get this job with no experience if you don't mind me asking? What did you do before?"

"My aunt got me the job. She knows the owner of the company. I never had a job before. This is my first job, and I went to college for lighting," Sandy informed.

"Oh, so your aunt got you the job. That's cool. What is lighting?" I asked with a curious face expression.

"You are funny. You don't know what lighting is? It's like the lighting for stages and stuff. It's people who adjust the lighting when you see a play or something. That's what I learned in college," Sandy advised.

"Nice. Well, let's get started. You can take your break at noon," I said as I started showing Sandy what to do.

"I have a question outside of the training if you don't mind?" Sandy asked in a hesitant tone.

"Sure, you can ask me anything. I'm an open book. I can tell you everything about this place?"

"How often do they give out raises? I was so surprised at the pay rate for this position. I mean, I know you make a lot more because you have experience, but I thought having a college degree would qualify me to get paid more," Sandy stated with a look of disgust.

"It's your second day, and you are already asking about raises, my kind of girl. They give the yearly cost of living raise, but of course, you can always sell yourself to get more. I sure do, every year."

"Oh, because making $19 an hour is pennies, and I don't know how long I'll be able to work here for that."

"You make what?" I asked in an appalled voice.

"I know, I know. That's terrible, right? Hopefully, they increase it soon. My aunt said once I learn the job, she will work on that for me," Sandy said with a hopeful smile.

"That's cool. Well, practice what I showed you and I'll be back shortly," I quickly rolled my chair back to my desk and power walked to my supervisor's office.

"Hey, Martha. Can I speak to you for a moment?" I asked my supervisor Martha.

"Sure, Sunni. Come right in."

"I can't train Sandy. I'm sorry, but this won't work. Please see if Tasha can train her."

"Oh, no. What happened? She seemed to be a sweet girl," Martha said with a confused look as she got up to shut her office door.

"She is a sweet girl. It's nothing personal towards her, but I can't train her, that's all. I'm going back to my desk now."

"Wait. There is no one else to train Sandy. You are a trainer now, and you get compensated for training. You have to tell me something," Martha stated with raised eyebrows.

"I can't train someone that makes $3 more an hour than me. The poor girl barely knew how to cut on the computer. I've been here for over five years, and someone can walk in the door making more than me, and you want me to train her?" I asked with attitude.

"First Sunni, it's unprofessional to talk about salaries. Secondly, she has a college degree, so you don't know her background," Martha said matter factly.

"Yes, she does have a college degree. In lighting! So, you telling me because she has a college degree, she walks in the door making more than an employee that's been here for over five years? Someone who knows this place in and out?" I said with anger.

"Yes, Sunni. Degrees get you a higher salary, no matter your experience. I'm sorry."

"Or is it who you know that gets you a higher salary no matter your experience?" I quickly asked.

"Sunni, come on, now you are being unfair. We can discuss your salary at raise time. For now, I need you to be professional, and please train Sandy."

"Sorry, I can't. I'm going back to school thanks to Sandy. I'll give you my resignation letter by the end of business today."

I quit that day. I walked with pride back to my desk. I wrote up a lovely resignation letter and put my two weeks' notice in to quit. The entire two weeks, I used the company hours to enroll in school, apply for financial aid, and research what trade I wanted to pursue. I knew I enjoyed billing because I liked numbers. I had started school once for Accounting but became so incredibly bored with numbers that I knew I didn't want to be an accountant. I decided to go back for Medical Billing and Coding. That way, no one could ever tell me education determined a salary and pay me pennies.

I told Kells that I quit, and he supported my decision to go back to school. He agreed to keep both kids during the day. Money got tight, and we only had one income. Whenever my money got low, I panicked. I felt like a failure, and it took me back to poverty days filled with lack. I was not in a functional mental space without my own money. I had to ask Kells for everything, and it drove me insane. He didn't mind because he was always an excellent provider for our family, but it made me feel awful. My mother kept reminding me that I was sacrificing so that I could give my family a better life. I was building a career, something to always fall back on.

Kells had me fucked up! His party behavior got worse and worse. Our fights escalated. We argued nonstop, but we still always found our way back to normalcy because we truly did love each other. We also kept our emotions together for the kids. He sat in the dining room on the desktop computer on the website MySpace. I was in the bedroom, and his phone sat on the dresser. It was on silent, but it kept lighting up. Our entire relationship this one number would call, but it was never locked under a name. I asked Kells about the number a few times, and he said it was a junkie's house around the way. He claimed everyone used her phone. I never trusted the phone number, until one day he answered it in front of me, and it was a guy on the other end. Since I heard a guy's voice, I stopped questioning the number.

I sat at the end of the bed, watching an old episode of "Living Single." Kells phone lit up again, and I got up to see who kept calling. It was that miscellaneous number. I put the phone down and ignored the light. I started to tell Kells someone was calling, but I chose not to. I watched the cell phone to see how many times the person would call. They called seven times, on the 8th time I answered.

"Hello. Who is this?" I asked straight to the point.

"Please put Kells on the phone," the remarkably familiar female voice asked.

"No. Kells is busy. Who is this?" I repeated.

"Girl, you know who it is," Destiny said with laughter.

"You can have him now. Good luck!" I hung up the phone and threw it at Kells' head. "Telephone for you!" I screamed.

"What the fuck you throwing shit at my head for?" Kells asked in an aggressive tone.

"All this time Kells, All this time! You have been messing with that girl all this time!" I yelled.

"What, girl? Why the fuck are you answering my phone? That's what we doing now?" Kells asked as he walked towards me.

"Fuck your phone. Fuck you! I knew it! I fucking knew it! That number never sat well with me. So that was her calling all that time, huh?"

"Fuck her! You are just trying to start shit. You don't even know why she was calling. She's young. She probably just said that to get under your skin."

"Well, you can take me out of the equation. I'm done with you. We are done! Get the fuck out!"

"Done? This my family. Ain't no done," Kells screamed.

"Oh, yeah. We are done. This is closure. I wish you well, Kells."

That was it; I couldn't take anymore. I asked Kells to move out. It wasn't an easy decision because I genuinely loved him, nor did he leave willingly. After two weeks of him returning unwanted, I had to call my father to help. Kells and my father had a beautiful relationship, so my father talked to him man to man and Kells left. My father even helped him move his stuff out to avoid conflict. I loved Kells, I really did, but I loved myself more.

I felt like Kells stabbed me in the back with the same knife repeatedly. I had two kids, no job, no babysitter, and no income. I was in school full time, and I was overwhelmed. I felt my world was crumbling down before me. Kells moved back downtown. He watched the kids when he felt like it but nothing like when we lived together. He tried to get me back a few times, but he eventually gave up and became the complete woman whore he so desperately desired to be. Kells did a lot of fucking! I once was at his apartment to pick up the kids and went to get Tira's bottle under his sink, and he had a box of 60 condoms, and half the box was already gone. He was getting it in!

Stand for something or fall for everything! I decided not to lay down with a dog and take the chance of getting fleas. I didn't make excuses for my mistakes. I simply chose not to share a man, the same way I chose not to train the privileged. I decided to be the one who makes noise, not the one who stays quiet. I didn't bow down with the other weak ones and pray for justice. I created my own justice, whether it was for a man or a job. I fought for what I believed in at all costs.

I didn't regret the years I spent with Kells because it was more good than bad, and I got my beautiful daughter out the deal, nor did I regret the years I spent at the job. I appreciated Webb's for teaching me the rules of the white privilege, which ultimately pushed me to further my education. I appreciated Destiny too for always hopping on Kells' dick, which eventually forced me to dodge a bullet. She prevented me from possibly making one of the biggest mistakes of my life. The mistake of giving my scorned heart to a BONOBOS!

CHAPTER 8

A PUERTO RICAN BLESSING

Sadly, for my kids, Kells was arrested a few months after our breakup, and he was sentenced to many years. Although we weren't together, I was devastated. I would be lying if I didn't admit how much I still loved him at the time. His arrest made me a real single parent. Marco was deceased, and Kells was gone to the system. My biggest struggle was to finish school. Kells was no longer around to watch the kids, and I immediately felt the effects of him being away. My entire support system went down the drain, financially and mentally. My family tried to step in and help as much as possible, but everyone worked during the day. I almost gave up on school, but God would always find a way for someone to watch them. It was an incredibly stressful time. I wasn't working, and the bills were piling up.

It came down to school or work once again. I had this same obstacle when I was 17 years old trying to finish high school. Here I was yet again in my early twenties experiencing the same challenges. The big difference this time was I had two kids that depended on me. I gave it to God. I decided not to quit school, and I started working part-time at a bookkeeping company. My old friend from Perkins helped me out whenever she could. I barely had money to pay her. I couldn't afford the bills anymore at my apartment, and my eviction was on the way. One of Kells homeboys name Bud owned a few properties over West Baltimore on Mosher Street.

Bud offered the kids and me a one-bedroom that he had available, and we moved in right before the sheriff arrived to kick us out. The master bedroom was huge, so I put the kid's bump beds on the side and my bed sat in the middle of the room. My kids and I were sharing a bedroom for the first time, and it killed my pride. My son always had his own bedroom since the day he was born. The apartment was in a horrible condition. The floors were torn up and barely standing. I bought tile to replace the disgusting carpet that the previous residents had destroyed. Home depot was my new favorite store. I learned how to lay tile and caulk up holes. I was a real handywoman. Bud didn't have time to fix up the place because we had to move suddenly, so I had to fix it. In return, he didn't charge me rent for the first few months. Bud hardly ever bugged me for rent at all. He knew I was struggling.

I hung out with my father every weekend. He was a manager at the mechanic shop called "Precise Tune." I started working there after school to make ends meet. I ran the front desk. I ordered car parts, handled the billing, and provided customer service for the customers. My father would let the kids stay in the shop sometimes while I was at school until my daughter lost a customer's keys. My father was pissed. the entire shop spent the entire day looking for the keys. She was a busy body and had too much energy to be at a workplace.

I was mentally, physically, financially, and emotionally in the worse place of my life. I was broke, living in a broken-down one-bedroom apartment with two kids, and driving an old ass Acura Legend. I was at my worse for sure. I was fighting for a better life but had to endure the struggle during the process. To top it off the Acura had some type of electrical issue, and it regularly died on me. The car was a lemon that squeezed all my energy and money. Every time I turned around, the piece of shit needed something, and yet it still left me on the side of the road.

It was Christmas time, and I went to Walmart to get all my kid's gifts. I had saved up money from working with my dad, and I started selling weed on the side just to survive. I shopped and shopped. I came out of Walmart to a tow truck, putting my car on the lift. I didn't scream or run after it. I knew the tags were expired, and I had two insurance violations. I didn't cry and say, *why me?* I simply looked at them take the piece of shit, and I felt a sense of relief. I didn't have a car anymore, but I didn't have the problems either. I called my mother to pick me up from the Walmart parking lot. Soon as I entered her car, we started talking.

"Sunni, I hate to see you having such a tough time. It's killing me," my mother said.

"I know, Ma. I don't know why things are always so hard for me. All I'm trying to do is be a good mother and finish school so I can provide for my babies. I'm just trying to live a decent life."

"I was surprised to see you so calm about losing the car. I thought you were going to be a crying disaster. You know we are crybabies," my mother joked.

"Honestly, Ma, I'm glad they took that Bitch. I was sick of that car taking all my damn money. At least I have my babies Christmas gifts," I said in an optimistic tone.

"How will you get to school in Towson with no car?"

"I don't know right now; it will all work out. I just need to finish school. I've lost too much already. I could've been got a job, and most of my problems would be gone, but that would mean I did it all for nothing. I can't quit now," I said.

"Yeah, you never quit. That's what we all admire about you. I will help any way I can, Baby. Just let me know," my mother said as she grabbed my hand.

"Thanks, Mommy. You know whatever I got, you got too. I will just be happy when this drought is over," I admitted.

My mother dropped me off, and I couldn't bring myself to open the front door. I sat in the hallway and just cried. I wasn't worried about the car; I was sad about my entire life. Poverty had taken over me with so much aggression. I somehow always had what I needed, but the penny-pinching lifestyle sent me into a deep depression. My daughter was going through a cry baby stage, and she was driving me insane. A few weeks later, I got called in by the school counselor at school, who told me I would have to repeat one of the classes because I missed more than two days of that course. I was devastated. That meant I wouldn't graduate on time, and I would have to take out another school loan just for that one class or pay for it out of pocket.

I went home and experienced the weakest day of my life. My daughter greeted me with tears, and my son asked for something from the store. The fact I had no money to give him and my daughter constant need for attention sent me over the edge. I never had a babysitter, even when people helped me that was for school, never for *me* time. I had my kids just about every day of their lives, and I was so overwhelmed. I sat at the end of the tub and shut the bathroom door. I reflected on my entire life. I thought of all the death and how hard it was for me to reach my next goal. I thought of my childhood and how things were continuing to get worse as an adult. I questioned why this life of poverty and death was the life God had chosen for me. I was sensitive and kind-hearted. Why did I have to experience so much pain? What was the cause?

As I thought harder, I cried harder, questioning *why I would even fight to live anymore. Why keep fighting a fight with a hopeless ending? Why fight a battle that can never be won?* I felt I was destined for hardship, and I would rather leave this place than to stay here in pain and poverty. Then I thought of my kids and cried harder. I thought how unfair it would be to leave them in such a shitty place with no guidance. My daughter cried louder, and I heard my son comforting her. I heard them both saying, "Mommy." Fuck it! Lights out!

I turned off the bathroom lights and grabbed my belt from around my waist and put it around my neck. I slowly stepped on the edge of the tub and turned away from the door. I placed the strap around the metal hook that hung above the shower rod, and I prayed this simple prayer, "God, I tried. I'm coming back to you. Please accept me. Amen." I removed my feet from the tub, and if I reached hard enough, my big toe could touch the floor. It only left me 2 inches to hang. I felt the pressure building up to my head, and it felt as if my brain was about to explode. I closed my eyes, and the first thing I saw was my Uncle Tom's face. His face traumatized me. His face was a reminder of how I felt when he killed himself in our apartment. His face reminded me of what I was about to do. I immediately opened my eyes and grabbed the rod to pull me up enough to stand back on the tub. I removed the belt from my neck and slowly fell in the tub. I laid there in a puddle of tears. I had lost all courage to fight for life, but I somehow found the strength to remove that belt from my neck.

I was not a mother that night. I did not feed my children dinner, nor did I ever open the bathroom door. I fell asleep on the cold tub floor; I felt horrible for being so weak. I woke up in the middle of the night to a freezing chill. My mouth had a pasty taste, and my eyes were crusty from dried up tears. I was so angry with myself for thinking about leaving my kids behind. I felt like pure shit. I walked to the living room and panicked because I didn't see the kids. I walked to the bedroom, checked both bump beds, and still didn't see the kids. I ran to my bed and ripped the covers off, and my kids were not there. I ran outside of the apartment, screaming their names through the dark empty streets. I banged on my upstairs neighbor's door, and she answered half-sleep. She informed me in a crackling voice that she hadn't seen them. My heart fell into my chest. My mind raced with fears and regret. I ran back into the apartment and looked under the bed and all over the room.

I started sweating, and I thought my kids left or were kidnapped. Maybe they thought I didn't want them and roamed the streets. Maybe someone took them. I screamed and screamed. When I finished yelling my guts out, I got quiet enough to hear a faint sound. I ran to the bathroom, and I saw my kids lying behind the bathroom door in the linen closet. They were hugging and wrapped up in towels. It broke my heart. They loved me so much that they fell asleep near the bathroom just to be close to me. I imagined the devastation they would've felt waking up to their mother's dead body.

I made my mind up at that very moment to never let life break me again. I would never be so weak as to take life so seriously to consider ending it. I decided to overcome all the bullshit life would throw at me. I would conquer this place and be fucking great. My kids would never grow up motherless and fatherless. I picked them up from the linen closet. I walked them to my bed and squeezed them tight. I kissed their faces repeatedly. The warmth of their bodies and the tightness of their hugs was all I needed to fight to stay alive. I vowed never to get so low to give up on life again.

I took out another loan for school and signed up to repeat the course against my wishes. Life didn't give a shit that I contemplated suicide, and things still got worse. My life had transformed into a state of survival. I had to fight for everything, and it repeatedly drained my spirit. Every so often, God threw in a blessing or maybe an Angel to help me through the rough times. This time the blessing name was Brooklyn. The day I met her was like any other ordinary day. I sat at the front desk of Precise Tune with dirty car parts that covered the counter. I was on the phone with the auto parts vendor complaining about the wrong part they sent.

My father was running the shop, and life was looking up for him. He called me outside, and I put up my finger to gesture to give me a minute because I was on the phone. When I got off the phone, I walked to my father's black Mercedes Benz. The wind was forcefully blowing. I had blonde extensions in my hair that blew with the wind. I noticed someone was in the car, and I walked to the passenger side to get a peek. A little light-skinned woman with a medium build jumped out the passenger side of the car. She had black people features but a different grain of hair that would portray that she was another race besides black.

"Oh my God, Desmond. She is freaking beautiful. Hey Mami," Brooklyn exclaimed in an excited tone.

"Hello. Thank you. How are you?" I responded with a smile.

"I'm great! You look just like your father. I'm Brooklyn, nice to meet you," Brooklyn said as she came to give me a bear hug as if we knew each other for years.

"Baby Girl. This is my new friend Brooklyn. We stayed up all night talking, and of course, I talked about you," my father explained.

"Oh, that's cool. When are you bringing your butt back to the shop? People have been complaining all day. Anyway, nice to meet you, Brooklyn. I have to get back to work," I said with a smirk while looking at my father.

"I'll be back by 2. I have to drop Brooklyn off first," My father yelled across the parking lot.

"Nice to meet you too, Mami. I'll be seeing you real soon," Brooklyn said eagerly as she hopped back in the Benz.

My father returned to the shop about an hour later. He was so excited about meeting Brooklyn. He said she was Puerto Rican, and she loved to cook. He said he couldn't wait for all of us to hang out. That Sunday, we all met at my father's house to watch the Ravens play football. Every Sunday, we picked a family member's home to watch the game; it happened to be my father's week. My dad had recently broken up with his old girlfriend only a week before I met Brooklyn. I walked into the house and smelled the most marvelous smell I had ever smelt. It was the smell of Puerto Rican cooking. My family was whispering and talking trash about who this new woman was in the kitchen cooking. They gossiped about how fast my father had moved on. They joked and called Brooklyn, my father's ex-girlfriend's name behind her back.

I was surprised to see Brooklyn at the Sunday football gathering. My family was also walking around whispering about me. They were curious to know if I was pregnant. Instead of asking, they just whispered, and it annoyed the fuck out of me. I was also tired of the slick remarks about Brooklyn. Although I didn't know her, she was friendly and kind enough to be cooking dinner for the entire family. The least they could do was respect her. I felt they could've grilled my father later in a more private setting. Brooklyn had a bold personality, and she did what the fuck she wanted to do. She stood in the kitchen no taller than 5 feet tall, making rice and beans with her Spanish music turned up to the max. I laughed at the sight of her dominant Puerto Rican personality. She didn't care that she was the new chick in my father's life. She only bothered to do what she wanted, and at the moment, all she wanted to do was cook dinner. I walked to the kitchen to greet Brooklyn.

"You got it smelling good in here. Do you need some help?" I asked as I looked around at all the food she had already cooked.

"Hey, Mami. Nope, I got the kitchen covered. How are you?" Brooklyn asked while stirring the sauce in a pot.

"I'm good. I can't complain. I'm a little hungry. Can I taste one of these fried bananas?" I asked bluntly.

"You are funny, Mami. They are called plátanos. Yup, take one, tell me if you like them."

"They are called plátanos! Mami take this!" my cousin Mason marked Brooklyn in a low voice as everyone laughed.

"What's so funny? Y'all been talking shit since I walked in here. Is there a problem?" I asked rudely.

"Well, excuse me, little Cuz, if we are thrown off by a new Spanish woman here one week after the last Spanish woman Marisel," Mason responded in a sarcastic voice.

"And so, what's the problem? Is she bothering all of you? Furthermore, I heard all y'all whispering about me being pregnant," I boldly stated.

"Little Cuz, I didn't say anything about you being pregnant," Mason said as he grabbed his drink off the table and took a sip.

"Maybe not you, but I heard the rest of y'all. So, I'll answer to stop all the gossip. I'm not pregnant, and if I were, that would be no one responsibility but mines. Anything else?"

"You need to take a chill pill. Sit your little ass down and have a drink," Mason implied.

"Give me a damn shot!" I demanded as I laughed along, still rolling my eyes at them.

Family can be intense, but at some point, you just have to laugh. I loved my older cousin Mason just as much as I loved my uncles. He was an agitator, and he often got under people's skin. Not mines, but he annoyed other people with his sarcastic personality. I was in a crappy mood, and sometimes family can truly get on your damn nerves. Brooklyn and Mason did not get along, and it started from their very first encounter. It was something about Brooklyn that was unique from the very first day I met her. She was different, and she demanded attention. She loved to cook, and she complimented me whenever she saw me. She made the people around her feel good with food or just love. Brooklyn had a New York style of dressing. I loved it when she put her shit on. Our relationship would grow in good and bad ways.

Three weeks went by, and life was truly kicking my ass. I went to my father's house, furious. When he opened the door, I immediately started screaming and crying about how completely fucked my life was. I had no babysitter, and finishing school seemed impossible. I had six weeks left, and every possible obstacle had come my way with full force. At the time, I didn't absorb the message of trying to be "Great." I soon learned you must fight to achieve anything that's more than ordinary, and soon as you are about to give up, a breakthrough usually comes. I continued my rant when Brooklyn came out of the room, appearing half-sleep as if I had woken her up.

"Mami, what's wrong?" Brooklyn asked with a blank stare.

"The girl who was watching the kids said she couldn't watch them anymore. She was an old friend, so she took a low payment. I could barely pay her on most weeks. Of, course no one will watch them for free," I vented.

"Calm down. How much longer do you have for school? What hours do you have to be there?" Brooklyn asked as she wiped the crust out of her eyes.

"I have exactly six weeks, and I go in the morning for pretty much all day," I answered.

"Listen, Mami. Everyone needs some help sometimes. My Titi Becka watched my kids for me all the time when they were younger. She taxed the hell out of me, but she did it. I will watch the kids for you," Brooklyn said as she walked to the kitchen.

"What? You barely know us. Did you hear me say, I can't afford to pay anyone?" I asked while walking behind her.

"I heard what you said. Did I ask you to pay me? Baby, it takes a village to raise kids. Just accept the blessing."

"Wow, I'm lost for words. I just don't even know what to say."

"Say, thank you. I'm only doing this because I see so much potential in you. I don't even think you know how special you are. I saw it on the very first day I met you. You are a go-getter and an amazing mother. I have never seen you without your kids, and that shows you are a bad La Puta."

"Thanks. You have no idea how much of a blessing you are to me right now. I appreciate you, and I'm happy you came into our lives," I said as I gave Brooklyn a big hug and many kisses all over her cheeks.

Every morning Brooklyn kept her word and opened their door and watched my two kids. Some mornings I would be banging for 15 minutes before she came to the door hungover and worn out from the party drugs her and my father partook in. She still opened the door, and I grew a deep love for her. The bond Brooklyn created with Tira was out of this world. She started speaking to her in only Spanish, and she loved her like her very first grandchild. She adored Zi too, but Brooklyn had four boys, so she gravitated more towards Tira because she was a new experience. Tira was also only nine months old, Brooklyn could influence her and mold her to the little Puerto Rican baby she wanted her to be. She called Tira, "Niña," and the rest was history.

I learned a lot about the Puerto Rican culture. The women are aggressive and a bit loca if I must say so myself. They love hard, and family is so important. With love, Brooklyn merged our families. One thing that shocked me was the versatile look of Puerto Ricans. They didn't all look like J Lo. Some of them were darker than my Black family, and their grains of hair varied. Most of them looked black, and some of them didn't. Our families blended perfectly together. We drove to Frederick, Maryland, to party with Brooklyn's family, and sometimes they came to Baltimore to party with us. Three of Brooklyn's sons lived in New York, and on occasion, we drove to see them too. That was our common interest; they loved family, and so did we.

Brooklyn and I often bumped heads. I was the Queen of my family. Although I was younger than my father, uncles, and cousins, I held a powerful impact on the family. They looked to me for guidance. Since my father and uncles lost their mother so young, I became the little mother of the family. I was the one who always cooked at our gatherings and made sure everything was together. The men would cook on the grill, but I did all the woman's duties. At first, I was ok with sharing the kitchen with Brooklyn, but then she just took over. She never let me cook, and we argued about the kitchen. I loved to cook just as much as she did, and it drove us both crazy. Speaking of taking over, Brooklyn took over everything. We were both bold, aggressive women, and for that reason, we often clashed. We loved each other as much as we couldn't stand each other at times. It was always more love than hate.

Brooklyn lived her life exactly how she wanted to, and rules did not apply in her reality. She took whatever she wanted, just like she took my father from Marisel. If Brooklyn wanted to make us a special seafood dish, she went right into the market, took every ingredient, and walked right out of the store. If we wanted to drink Grey Goose, she went right in the liquor store and grabbed a half gallon and walked right out of the store. If she wanted a specific job, she lied about her credentials and got the job. Her bad girl, New York style, was attractive, and her not giving a fuck attitude is what made me love her and despise her.

My entire life, I heard darker black women complain about their complexion. Not complain like they didn't want to be dark but complain about how society treated dark women. They would say guys liked lighter women, or someone had it easier because they were lighter, or they had to fight growing up because they were called dark and ugly. I grew up with a beautiful black Queen, and my dark mother never talked about complexion in our house. Lighter skin had no value in my mind, and I would of much preferred to get some of my mother's chocolate. People love to be victims and fall into a pity role because of their insecurities. NEWS FLASH! Light skinned women had the same obstacles. We had to fight because we were light or because someone thought we wanted their man, or for just being light-skinned. That's what Brooklyn and I experienced on this ugly day. My father gave us some money, and we drove to West Baltimore to a hole in the wall called "Great Times." We sang and danced with each other. We had fun in our own little world, but the stares in the lounge from the women screamed hate and envy. A girl bumped me hard, and I continued to dance instead of confronting her. I was tipsy, and I chose to assume it was a mistake.

"Excuse you!" Brooklyn yelled to the thick girl who bumped me.

"No! I don't excuse myself for no Bitches," the thick girl replied.

"Bitches?" Brooklyn hollered.

"Come on, B. Fuck her!" I said as I grabbed Brooklyn's arm, pulling her back to the dance floor.

"These little young Bitches better be lucky," Brooklyn went on to fuss as I freaked her to get her back in a good mood.

"We here for fun. Don't worry about her, plus ain't you like 50?" I joked. "You know these Baltimore chicks love to be angry for no reason. You want another drink?" I asked, still dancing, and sipping from my cup.

"Yeah, I need a drink to calm my nerves," Brooklyn stated, still looking frustrated.

I walked to the bar section to order us two more drinks. The guys were on me and flirting like crazy. We barely paid for any drinks that night. Had I been with my friends, I probably would've smacked the girl for being disrespectful, but I was with Brooklyn, and she was like a mother to me. I didn't want anyone putting their hands on her, she was older, and I wanted to avoid conflict for the sake of Brooklyn. I knew we were in their hood, and it was quite a few of them. Brooklyn and I continued to drink and dance.

As the night dwindled, we completely forgot about the petty bump that happened earlier that night. Here's where the night took a complete turn for the worse. Brooklyn was extremely tipsy at this point, and she was laughing and not paying attention. I slowed down to observe the room, and the vicious looks on a group of females' faces were alarming. I stupidly ignored it. They had no reason to be upset. I wasn't dating any of the guys, and I didn't know any of the women. The lights came on in the lounge as the DJ screamed "Last Call," over the mic. We started to make our way out of the lounge; the line was long. I stood in the line rapping along with Young Jeezy, "Lose My Mind."

"Why y'all tripping, I'm just fine,
12:45, bout that time,
Couldn't get it all week, time to unwind
Drink like a tank, lose my mind,
This shit crazy, way too bad
Rosé baby, waste two stacks
Hottest thing in the lot, that there mine
Can't spell sober, lost my mind."

It was one of my favorite songs and I sung it as I did a tipsy two step. My swag and hype way of rapping along with Jeezy's song annoyed the group of ladies who stood on the other side of the line. They stood glaring at me like vultures that patiently waited for their prey. I searched the crowd for the girl who bumped me earlier so I could be on point, but she was no longer in the lounge. I continued to sing, and dance as the line slowly moved towards the exit. I relaxed a little because I didn't have to be so alert since the threat from earlier was nowhere in sight. One of the girls from the crew across from us in the line kept throwing indirect comments.

"I hate light-skinned Bitches! They always think they all that," a thick dark girl said.

"They sure do! That is until someone knocks them off their high horses. You feel me?" another girl asked.

"Hell yeah, I feel you. We don't like new Bitches coming around here anyway," the thick girl replied.

"Brooklyn, you on point?" I leaned over and whispered to Brooklyn.

"Yeah, Mami. That piece of trash from earlier left out with a guy," Brooklyn said with no emotion.

"No, I'm talking about these chicks across from us!" I informed her.

Brooklyn missed the remarks, so she had no idea what I was talking about. Finally, we were out of the lounge. The fresh air was refreshing. The moment it hit my face, I felt free and grateful to be out of the closed-in space. Brooklyn and I laughed and talked as we walked over to the Cadillac Escalade, that my father loaned us. We wanted to sit up high, so my father let us take it for the night. We stood in between the driver door with the door open, which blocked our view from the opposite side.

"Wait, Mami. Let's stand out here so I can smoke a cigarette before we get in the truck," Brooklyn suggested.

"Shit, give me one too. I feel good. Those drinks were on point," I chimed in.

"We need to get some food now, so we don't get sick," Brooklyn said as she took a hail off her cigarette.

Before I could respond, I was unexpectedly caught off guard with a weak ass punch to my jar. I took a few seconds to say to myself, *I know this Bitch didn't just hit me with that weak ass punch.* The punch felt like a hit from Tira. It was so faint and pathetic. I had to laugh before I start putting in work. Two girls were fighting me, and three girls were on Brooklyn. We both were caught off guard, and we couldn't see them coming from behind the truck doors to even prepare for a fight. Brooklyn and I both stood on our two feet as we got jumped by some haters just because we were light-skinned.

The fight took a horrible turn for the worse when I saw the 3rd girl pull Brooklyn down by her hair. I continued to fight to get the two girls off me, and my entire goal was to avoid hitting the ground. I glanced over and saw Brooklyn's body hit the concrete, and she was bringing one of the girls down with her, something snapped, *Oh, fuck no! I can't let them stomp Brooklyn.* I'm not sure where the strength came from, but I blacked out, and I started beating Bitches up. I had to get Brooklyn off the ground. I dusted off the weak link that was fighting me and thank God a guy came and pulled the other girl away. I was now free to take care of two of the girls fighting on Brooklyn, and that's precisely what I did.

Brooklyn jumped back on her feet, and we finished off the last three standing. We were so caught off guard that it took us a minute to build up the anger to put in work. The beginning of the fight, my mindset was, don't get on the ground and get at least one of them off of you. At the end of the battle, my mindset was, teach these Bitches don't ever play with you. The possibility of Brooklyn getting stomped was the anger I needed. One of the guys that were buying us drinks in the lounge came to break up the fight at the perfect time. We were all getting tired except Brooklyn; she was ready to rumble all night if need be. The girls were screaming angry remarks as the men pulled them away.

"You Bitches are weak. I'm still pretty!" I said as I fluffed my hair out and looked at my face on the side mirror.

"Yup, Mami. They didn't do shit," Brooklyn added as we both laughed hysterically.

"I can't believe we just got jumped," I laughed.

Brooklyn had a small bruise on her nose, and I had a long scratch across my entire neck. That was all the damage they had done. We both laughed and talked about the fight during the ride home. We handled ourselves, but it was one of the dumbest fights I had ever had. It wasn't my first time being attacked because of my complexion. It always humored me how people would assume I was stuck up, or I thought I was better before ever having a conversation with me. They assumed I would be so self-centered that I would be glued in a mirror all day when the truth is, I barely looked in mirrors.

Complexion or looks never really crossed my mind until someone else mentioned it. As a kid, I never saw color. I thought all people were the same. I thought my mother and I were the same complexion. It wasn't until a little boy down Perkins kept calling me, "Redbone" did I ever recognize color. I went home that day and asked my mother, "What is a Redbone?" She said, "Who called you that dumb ass shit?" I told her what the boy said. She explained I was light-skinned because I got more of my father's complexion, but it didn't mean anything. I never thought of it again. Society never let me forget. Throughout my life, it felt like I was tortured for being lighter. It was mainly females who had an issue, and the only time guys would be disrespectful is if I wasn't interested in them. My teenage conversations with guys usually went something like this...

"Hey, Shorty! Shorty! Damn, you can't stop walking for a minute?" he would aggressively state.

"Hey. I'm good Babe, I'm in a rush," I would politely brush them off.

"Well, fuck you then! You stuck up light-skinned Bitch!"

"Fuck you too!" I would yell with my middle finger up.

Yup, that was a normal disrespectful interaction from a ruthless guy who didn't even know me. At one point, I was grateful that I didn't have a big butt or big boobs because I disliked the negative attention I received from boys. I got cursed out quite a few times in my life just for walking down the street. Boys and their egos! They can't stand rejection.

The crazy stories and situations Brooklyn and I encountered are endless. Brooklyn was an adventure. She took my father to hell and back with drama and love. She was the reason I finished school. She was the best cook ever, and she fed us with so much love. She was my kids, Abuela. She was my biggest cheerleader. She was the only woman I fought and loved so hard. She was my father's weakness and my daughter's strength. Brooklyn was our Puerto Rican Blessing. A blessing could be considered God's favor and protection. A blessing shouldn't be taken for granted, nor should you think God's favor will always be around.

CHAPTER 9

STREET RATS

When you think you are at your lowest, there's a possibility you could go lower. There are moments in life that you must fall so far down so you can feel the grit, the pain, the suffering, and the humiliation. If you don't feel it, you can't possibly know how good it feels to be at the top. You can't appreciate the strength you endure from the hardcore lessons unless you go through them. Some people were fortunate enough to skip the pits of life. Some people didn't skip hardship, but they chose not to grow and learn from it. Me, on the other hand, I didn't get to skip any of life's hardships. I had to take one slow horrifying step at a time. I never skipped one step on the latter of life. This period of my life is the lowest of the levels. It's where you are so low that the street rats could bite you. You are beneath the cement, and you must fight through the concrete before you can even see the first step. Oh, Bitch, I'm fighting! I will reach the top, but first, I must get out of the pits.

The pits are where I lived on Mosher Street. I had reached a new low. This low was not just about poverty. This stage of my life was about, "The Fight." It takes real courage to fight against all odds, to fight against your environment, and to fight against what some would say is destined for you. I wanted so much more, but I was surrounded by people who were content and wanted nothing more than what their eyes allowed them to see.

I only spoke to my neighbors and the lady at the corner store. West Baltimore was always so foreign to me. Although I equally lived on both sides, I never quite got the rules of how the Westside worked. To my surprise, after I finished school, I didn't just get a job right away. I spent all my money getting to interviews, where I was always told I didn't have enough experience. I never understood how the jobs expected you to have so much experience if you are just finishing school with a new career. Where did those employers expect you to get all this experience from if no one allowed you to work? The struggle of finding work as a Medical Biller and Coder was a burden. I had already been through hell and back to finish school, and now I couldn't find a job.

I sat on the front steps with a bottle of Moscato wine. I watched the guys on the dirt bikes ride up and down the street. Some of the guys used one hand; others would be popping a wheelie while never letting the bike down. It was always interesting to watch the dirt bike boys ride their bikes. The hood is consumed with noise. It becomes normal to hear helicopters, dirt bikes, loud music from cars, firecrackers, people yelling, or even gunshots. My apartment sat right across from the police station. It always confused me how so much crime went on right in front of the precinct.

An older guy name Earl came over to talk. Earl was dark with poppy eyes and ashy skin. He lived in an abandoned house across the street. The outside of the house was missing bricks from the design, and the concrete steps were cracked. Every time they walked up the steps, they took the risk of the steps sinking in. I never went inside his house, but I knew they didn't have electricity. Earl walked across the street with a limp and a fast pace. He used a branch from a tree to hold himself up, which took the place of a cane.

"Hey, Little Mama, what you got? What you need?" Earl asked.

"Hey, Earl. What you need?" I asked.

"I need three dollars, and I got two bars of Dove soap. I can give you both for 3," Earl replied.

"That's not a deal, Earl! The bars are only a dollar apiece in the stores."

"Well, shit, what you want then?" Earl asked with a disappointed look.

"Earl, you are a mess. Give me both bars of soap for two dollars, and I will give you another dollar for walking to the liquor store for me. Is that cool?" I asked as I negotiated with my last $10 bill.

"Yes, Ms. Sunni. That's cool with me. What do you want?" Earl asked as he did a drunk man's dance.

"Get me another bottle of Moscato like this. I had a rough day," I laughed at his offbeat dancing as I lifted the bottle of wine to show him my brand.

"I'm not sure what's going on with you, but whatever it is, you will get through it. You are a strong young woman and an amazing mother. We always say how we admire how much you love those kids."

"Thanks, Earl. I do love my babies. Oh shit! Did you see those sparks coming from the side of the building?" I asked in a panicked tone.

"Hell yeah. Get your kids out of there if they home," Earl said in a frantic tone.

"The kids are not home. They are spending the weekend with my father. I'm a need that wine sooner than later. Knock on the door when you get back."

I ran upstairs, skipping two steps at a time. The hallway was pitch dark, and all the lights were out. I grabbed a flashlight and looked around to make sure the sparks didn't cause a fire anywhere. Now the apartment didn't have electricity as if things couldn't get any worse. I decided not to break down but instead go back on the steps and drink another bottle of wine. I heard Earl's big mouth around the corner, and I felt a sense of relief to know he was near. I seriously needed a drink.

"Was everything good in the house?" Earl asked as he handed me the bottle of wine.

"Nothing was burning, but now the lights are out. I will call the electric company in the morning. Tonight, just fuck it," I said as I hunched my shoulders.

"Yeah, sometimes you just have to say, fuck it. I'm a sit here and drink my beer with you if you don't mind."

"Of course, I don't mind. You love that beer. Look at those rats just running back and forth. They are huge!"

"I know. I hate them, motherfuckers! Make sure you move your car every night because they will chew your wires. Never park in the same spot."

"My car got towed a few weeks ago. I've been riding rentals or cars from my father's shop."

"Well, no car, no worry from them scavenger ass rats. I'll see you tomorrow, God willing!" Earl said as he smashed the 211 Steel Reserve beer can and threw it in the gutter.

Earl limped across the street, and I continued to sit on the steps to finish my wine. I didn't want to go into the dark apartment; however, the view of the rats running from one curb to the other was excruciating. I wanted to escape my reality and just wake up on an island somewhere. I tried to stay in the dark apartment but couldn't bear the sight of all darkness. I decided to catch a sedan to Licia's house. I knew I would have fun and leave my worries behind. The kids were gone, and the house was dark, so it was no need to stay there alone. Soon as I arrived at Licia's house, everyone was so happy to see me.

"What's up? You good?" Licia asked.

"Yeah, I'm good friend. I just had a rough day. I got some grass, do you have blunts?"

"You already know I got blunts. Don't act brand new!" Licia laughed.

"Dag, it looks different in here. I like your new TV and stuff," I said while looking around Licia's apartment.

"Thanks. I had to upgrade some stuff. Remember I told you about the dude Nico? I told you he was hot, and he looked like your type."

"Yeah, I remember. I never met him, though. You need help cooking?"

"I got that pot of greens from Mrs. Nessa, but they don't taste like nothing. Can you do something with them?" Licia asked while looking in the pot.

"Yup. You know me! I can make something happen. Why you bring up Nico?" I asked with a curious face.

"Hold that thought, let me get the door," Licia said as she left the kitchen.

I started looking through Licia's seasoning cabinet while she slowly walked to the door. I heard her open the front door. I peeked my head around the kitchen corner and saw a handsome, tall treat standing in the doorway. He had a caramel brown complexion, a gentle smile with golds on his top teeth, and pretty pink gums. He had swag; he wore a white long sleeve thermal designer shirt under a puffy army green color vest, a pair of army fatigue pants with big pockets, a gold chain around his neck, and a fresh pair of butter Timberland boots. His hair was freshly braided. His swag and style were unique. He didn't look like the regular around the way guys. I could tell he was from over West. Guys over West always had more style than the Eastside dudes. I wanted to run to the bathroom and fix myself up. Then I told myself, *girl chill. You don't even know who that is. He could be Felicia's friend. Don't be thirsty*! Licia snapped me out of my thoughts.

"Sunni! Come here, real quick," Licia yelled from the living room as her and the guy stood close to the front door talking.

"Yeah. Girl, I brought those greens back to life. Wait until you taste them now," I said with excitement as I walked towards them both.

"Nico, this is Sunni and Sunni this is Nico," Licia smirked before walking away. She completely disregarded my comment about the food.

"So, you're the famous Nico. Nice to meet you," I said, looking him up and down.

"I don't know about all that," he said in a humble tone with a slight blush on his face.

"Licia been saying we should meet for months. What area do you live in?" I asked Nico admiring his watch.

"I live over West. Yeah, we kept missing each other. Are you going to take my number? I have to make a run."

"I guess I can take your funky number," I joked. Nico smiled, and we exchanged numbers. We talked for about fifteen minutes before he left.

"Bitch! Get out here! He is Hot!" I screamed to Licia.

"I told you! Y'all complement each other well. I knew he was your type," Licia said as she smoked the blunt.

"Hell yeah, he's my type. Why you been hiding his ass? Get the scoop and tell me what he thought."

"He comes through like once a week. You already know I'm a tell you everything," Licia said as she took another hail off the blunt.

"How soon you think I should text him? I'm not trying to look pressed," I said anxiously.

"Look at you blushing. I knew you were going to like Nico. I don't know, text him tomorrow," Licia said as she hunched her shoulders.

"Fuck it. I'll wait a few days. Yeah, good looking on that one. Pass the blunt," I said with my hand pointed in her direction.

I woke up the next morning on Licia's couch. I called the electric company, who said they couldn't send anyone out until that Monday. Licia offered me to stay over until I got everything situated. I declined and decided to just spend the day with her. I had to pick up the kids Sunday night from my father's, but after I told him about the sparks and the lights going out, he told me to leave the kids with him. I forgot about all the issues I was having. I let my mind rest. Whenever I was around good people, or surrounded by love, I always felt better. I left Licia's house that Saturday night and went to my father's house to have Sunday dinner. Brooklyn was in the kitchen, cooking and swaying her hips to the music my father had blasting.

"Wow, Brooklyn! You outdid yourself again. Who is going to eat all this food?" I asked while looking around the kitchen.

"You know I love my family, Mami. Come taste this new sauce I made," Brooklyn said with a wooden spoon in her hand.

"That's good. I secretly think you want all of us to be 500 pounds the way you be cooking," I said with a smirk.

"My grandbabies helped me cook. They wanted different things, so I cooked everybody's favorite dish," Brooklyn said as she closed the oven door.

"It smells good. How much longer? You know you feed us like 2 O'clock in the morning from too much cooking."

"I'm only waiting on the fish. Put one of my songs on Mami."

"You want, Una Vaina Loca?" I asked while fumbling with my phone.

"Yup. Put that on, so me and my Nina can dance while we cook," Brooklyn said as she grabbed Tira's hands.

Tira and Brooklyn danced to her Spanish music, and we all laughed and sung along. The next morning, I went back home to deal with the electrical issue. The Electrician told me there was an issue in the building's barbershop area, and the entire building would have to be rewired by the landlord. I called Bud, who said that wasn't something he could do at the time. He wasn't even making money off the building. The barbershop was closed, and at the time, I was the only other tenant. I rarely could afford to pay the full rent, if I paid it at all. I understood where Bud was coming from, so I went to the streets for help. I paid a guy to cut the lights back on. It was $150. He said he could only cut on half of the building for safety reasons. Half was better than none. All the lights in my apartment worked except the bathroom. I just dragged a lamp from the kitchen whenever we needed a lot of light in the bathroom. Mostly since it was just my kids and me, we left the bathroom door open for light.

The electrical issue caused more problems than my mind could comprehend. Every few weeks, the electric company was cutting the lights back off, which was the start of a major headache. I had finally reached out to Nico, who didn't live far from me. We started hanging out a lot. Nico was fly but humbled. He wasn't big-headed, and he had a sense of struggle embedded in his personality. We talked for hours about everything. We were both project babies as we called it. We realized we knew some of the same people, and that connected us more. What attracted me to Nico the most was his lack of judgment. He never judged. He came to my house and acted as if he was in a mansion.

He always complimented my cooking, and he appreciated the small things. He made me feel special, not on my best days, but on my most basic days. He admired my rough days. Holey T-shirt, cleaning up with bleach, hair slicked back, no makeup kind of days. We had no titles; we just enjoyed each other's company. He didn't ask me questions, and I didn't ask him questions. We mutually respected each other's space. The day I gained a new level of respect for Nico was on a cold day when the unexpected happened. Nico called to come over, and I told him I would be home in an hour. When I arrived home, it was to my surprise the lights were out again. I fell apart. I still couldn't get a job after all the sacrifices I made to finish school. Not to mention, the electrical issue took so much of my money, and yet the lights were off again. Nico walked in the dark hallway of the building.

"Yo! You in here?" Nico yelled up the steps.

"Yeah, I'm here. I tried to call you to tell you don't come, but my cell phone died," I said in a low whimpering tone.

"Are you crying?" he asked.

"No! I'll call you when everything gets straight," I said while sniffling.

"Your punk ass is crying. I'm coming up there!" Nico yelled from the bottom of the dark building steps.

"I ain't no punk," I said as I wiped my tears and handed him a flashlight.

"We been through too much with our hard project lives to be crying and shit from some lights. I thought you were from down Perkins?"

"Shut up. Shit just been fucked up for months. You know how much money I've paid to keep these lights on?"

"And? What are you going to do about it now? Falling apart won't cut them bitches back on. What you need?" he asked with a firm face.

"I don't know. I feel like giving up! Everything is so damn hard," I said in a frustrating tone.

"Look, I'm not sitting with you in the dark while you talk that pity stuff. Come on, let's get some extension cords and get a neighbor to hook that shit up for tonight. That way, you won't have to worry about the wires. Figure the rest out tomorrow," Nico said sternly.

"What's in that bag? Let's take a drink first," I said as I started to pull myself together.

"That's right. Get your shit together. Take a drink and calm down."

Nico and I sat in the dark for two hours, talking about life. He acted as if the lights were on. He was utterly unfazed by my struggles. I gained so much respect for him that day. We eventually got up and went to the 24-hour Rite-Aid, and he bought me extension cords to use my neighbor's electricity. We had great sex that night. Nico liked me, and I liked him, but he always made it a point to remind me we weren't in a relationship. I never pretended we were. I had so much going on in my life that a relationship was far from my radar. I needed a job, electricity, a new place, and a car. A man was far from my goals.

Nico was smooth and a mystery to my clouded mind. He met me at a very damaged time in my life, and his laid-back personality let me explore poverty from a different mindset. He was an awesome reminder that I could overcome anything because I had overcome everything. Nico and I had no strings attached, just simply good sex, wisdom, and friendship. Our friendship ended when the slip up happened. When our luck ran out, and some sperm met some egg and decided to collide. Apparently, the pull-out method doesn't always work. As if things couldn't get more complicated, well, they did.

I looked at my two fatherless kids. I promised them a good life, and I couldn't let them down. I aborted Nico's child. I selfishly chose to provide for the two kids I already had and decided not to bring another human in my world. I didn't even have the decency to tell Nico. I just woke up, made an appointment to the abortion clinic, and walked in the waiting room alone and numb. I kept telling myself it was only a fetus, and I was making the right decision. I laid on a cold operating bed in a small room with dimmed lights as a machine sucked someone's life right out of my uterus. There were many girls at the abortion clinic, which felt alarming. It was no possible way I could know every woman's situation or understand how they got to the abortion clinic to make that choice. I did know one thing, we all had a hard decision to make, and some humans would never see the light of day based on our choices. I felt empty after the abortion and I realized it wasn't just a fetus, it was me and Nico's child.

Nico later found out from Licia's boyfriend. To my surprise, he denied us. He rejected the possibility he could've got me pregnant, although we both knew we broke all the "protected sex" rules. Nico went away, and our friendship was over. I was hurt, but I also knew we both handled the situation completely wrong; either way, that would be the end of us dating in that decade. We were young, and we both moved on with our lives. Whenever we saw each other, there was still always a feeling of comfort. I often thought of him, and he randomly reached out to me over the years. I would always start off being rude to him, but then his smile would eventually calm my spirit, and all would be forgiven.

I walked across the street one day to go to the corner store. As I stood in the doorway of the crowded store, I noticed the unbelievable amount of street rats that ran from building to building. I watched the cars drive down Mosher Street, and each vehicle ran over one big fat dead rat that had been hit earlier that day. The rats were bold! They started coming out in the daytime, and you never knew where they were hiding. They would be hiding under some car, some alley, or some gutter. I watched them in disgust as they ran like the sneaky Vikings they were.

I had never seen a rat up close, and I never wanted to. I had no intention of building an understanding of how a rat operates. I remember a few years prior; I watched a movie called, "The Women of Brewster Place." There was a scene where the actress slept with her baby, and a rat jumped on the bed. She panicked and grabbed her child and left in the middle of the night. I remember thinking, *That's right! Get the hell out of there!* Throughout my life as an adult, I had one very annoying flaw. This flaw would cause me so much pain. It was the reason I didn't hug Marco tight the night he died. That flaw was the power of "My Pride."

I had a lot of pride. I was on my own since I was 17 years old, and there was nothing I wouldn't do to keep my independence. It was all I had left after all I had been through. My biggest flaw was tested on this day. It was the day I met a street rat, face to face. It was a cold night, and I laid in my king-sized bed with my kids. My big beautiful cat named Smurf laid comfortably on the bottom of the bed in a curled-up fetus position. My kids were sound asleep, and my mind was racing. I tried to fall into a deep sleep, but my constant thoughts forced me to lay in a cycle of exhaustion. I laid in the bed with my eyes closed, reflecting on how I let my life get so fucked up.

I squeezed my eyes tight in the hopes of finally dosing off. With no luck, I decided to count myself to sleep. I slowly started counting, "One, two, three, four." My counts were interrupted by the sound of a squeak. My cat, Smurf, immediately jumped off the bed and ran to the living room. I heard loud noises of "Squeak, Squeak, Squeak." I panicked because the sounds were so bold, and they sent a chill through my body. The squeak was more aggressive than a mouse, and the vibrations of the tone echoed through the apartment. I tried to convince myself it was just a mouse. Reality would soon set in, and I would soon be meeting a fucking Rat.

Smurf ran through the house with force. He ran like a heavy foot man, and the floor seemed to be shaking. I heard things in the living falling to the floor, picture frames, pillows, and other random objects. I then listened to a deafening squeal. My stomach turned into knots, and I dreaded what awaited me in the morning. My cat Smurf slowly walked back into the bedroom with a look of satisfaction on his face as he jumped back on the bed. He laid back in his same spot; however, now he was alert. He was no longer comfortably lying in a fetus position. He was ready for war. We both laid there uncomfortably in complete awareness and alertness.

I was afraid to approach the living room and find whatever Smurf had killed. A rat will always be

179

exposed, and this rat would be no different. I got up from my bed, shut my bedroom door, and finally found a way to fall asleep. I woke up before my kids, and I realized the night before wasn't a dream. I slowly opened the bedroom door and looked around. I didn't see anything dead on the floor, so I immediately felt a sense of relief. I thought, *maybe Smurf didn't kill anything, and I wouldn't have to wake up to another day filled with bullshit.* I picked up the items that had fell while Smurf chased whatever, and I continued to walk in the kitchen to head to the bathroom.

I tiptoed around, making sure to observe my surroundings. As soon as I entered the kitchen, I saw an exceptionally long tail, much longer than a mouse. I jumped back out of fear. There was only one way to the bathroom, and meeting the rat was my only option if I wanted to pee. He laid there big and dead. I had three immediate options. I could grab my kids and run like the lady on "The Women of Brewster Place," I could pee on myself, or I could run and get someone to pick up the rat. I didn't pick either option. I chose to deal with the rat and so I mentally prepared to jump over it. My skin was crawling, and my adrenaline was pumping with anxiety. I looked at the rat, and to my surprise, it had enormous ears and almost like see-through nails, and it creeped me out even more.

I made the jump, and thankfully the rat was dead, and he didn't jump with me. I went to the bathroom, and as bad as I had to pee, the urge to vomit came out first. I gagged my entire stomach line out, and then I screamed, a loud scorching scream. I was at a breaking point, and screaming was my temporary relief to avoid insanity. My life was in complete chaos, and I felt the rat took me to the gutter. I knew when I got out of the bathroom; the rat would still be there to remind me of how fucked up my life was. After 10 minutes of screaming and crying, I got the courage to open the bathroom door. There the rat laid waiting to drag me down so low. I would be lower than the cement thanks to the fucking Rats.

I slowly walked back to the kitchen; I closed my eyes and jumped back over the rat. It was the worse jump of my life. I didn't know if it would move or if I would trip and find myself on the floor with the rodent. I ran to get Mr. Earl before my kids could see the disgusting intruder that had invaded our shitty apartment. Mr. Earl limped over with his stick cane and informed me that they too had rats. The block was pretty much infested from all the vacant properties. I gave him $5 to pick up the rat. I only had $10 in cash and barely knew where my next dollar would come from. I was falling apart, and only my Queen could get me back on track, so I called my mother. She picked up the phone on the first ring.

"Hey, Ma. What are you doing?" I asked in a disturbed tone.

"Nothing, I'm about to get ready for work. What's wrong with you?" My mother instantly asked.

"Nothing, I'm okay," I replied quietly.

"No, you are not. You've been on my mind heavy this morning, and I know you, Sunni. So, what's wrong?" my mother repeated in a worried tone.

"I don't want to tell you because I know you will freak out, and I'm freaked out enough. I just wanted to hear your voice," I said in a low tone.

"Sunni, just tell me. Whatever it is, we can work it out. You are my only child. I'll do anything for you," my mother said in a sympathetic tone.

"Smurf killed a rat. A fucking rat. I'm shaking right now. Why is this happening to me?"

"Oh, my God! Sunni, get my grandbabies, and come down here now! You sure it was a rat?"

"Yes, I'm sure. I see the nasty bastards run across the street all the time. We will be okay, Mommy. I'm a get, someone, to patch the apartment up so they can't get in," I said in an insecure tone.

"No, fuck that, Sunni. You need to leave. I know I only have a one-bedroom apartment, but we will make it work. Please just leave," my mother pleaded.

"Ma, I know you don't understand, but if I lose my independence and become enabled, I will go into a deep depression. I've had my own place since I was 17. I don't think I can mentally handle that."

"You always have so much pride. Maybe God wants you to slow down and stack your money. You won't have to pay for anything with me. It will allow you to get back on your feet," my mother said in a convincing tone.

"I'll think about it, but for now, I need Mr. Cole to patch these holes for me," I said, disregarding her request.

"Sunni, are you crazy? We are talking about rats, and the lights are going off every few days anyway. Just put your pride aside and come here. At least do it for the kids," she pleaded.

"Ma, please don't push. Can you bring Mr. Cole up here when you get off?"

"I guess Sunni. Yeah, I'll bring him. I love you, and you are not alone."

I got off the phone with my mother feeling awful. I knew I should've left the apartment that day. To me, leaving meant I had fallen off even worse than where I was. I knew my mother loved me, and it was killing her watching me, and her grandkids live in those conditions. Mr. Cole came later that day and patched up every hole in the apartment. I still felt uneasy, but I managed to fall asleep. A few nights later, I was awakened to the sound of rats playing in the ceilings. Over the next few weeks, Smurf had killed three more rats. They chewed through everything, and they would take over as the rodents they were. I got a job offer that paid the same amount the privileged white girl's salary was at the job I left. The universe had a sense of humor. I got two paychecks and decided to take my mother up on her offer. The kids and I moved in with my mother.

The day we moved out of the apartment, the floor caved in, and my Uncle Charlie fell through. Luckily, he didn't fall all the way through, but he fell enough for us to laugh at the poor conditions I was living in. For the first time ever, it was funny. Those rats took me to a new low, and I'm glad I felt the grit. Something unknown mentally happened to me in that apartment. My circumstances were molding me into a fucking beast. I would know life and poverty so I could be that GREAT one day. I didn't experience those conditions for sympathy or pity. I experienced them so I could truly feel the bottom so I could enjoy the journey to the top.

Life is about your perception, and rats are considered to be the most feared rodents. I looked down on rats and despised the sight of them. I was forced to face a rat in the comfort of my home, and I thought I could go no lower than a face to face visual of a street rat. I researched rats later in life, and learned rats are worshipped in certain Indian traditions. Rats are sensitive and shy. They can't handle peer pressure, which is why they follow the other rats even if they are not doing something pleasing. Rats love to play, and they make laughter sounds, which brings them so much joy. They have excellent memories, and they can become depressed if they are forced to be alone. Lastly, they are brilliant. Yes, I experienced the gutter where I was left to jump over rats, and that jump should only be perceived as an experience. A street rat is the most feared rodent, but it shouldn't be. What comes next for my life was the real fear I would soon have to face.

CHAPTER 10

AN OLD FLAME

A fire burns hot, and the red flames are so sexy and tempting. There's an excitement in watching a fire burn. There's also fear of the unknown. How long will the fire burn, and how much damage will the start of a flame cause? The flames are daring and hypnotizing. Watching the smoke flare in the air with a mist of roughness is powerful. Finding yourself involved with an old flame that has already been burned out is dangerous. The heat is a threat to the heart, but it comes with warmth. All fires must burn out, no matter how big or small, and sadly all that is usually left from such an intriguing flame is an unattractive pile of debris.

Moving in with my Queen would, for sure, be a challenge. My mother only had a one-bedroom apartment. My two kids slept on a futon near my mother's dining room. I slept with them, or I would sleep on the couch. My mother was so supportive and tried to make us feel as comfortable as possible. As much as it killed her, she decided not to nag. The adjustment was hard for her, too. She was not used to sharing her space with another woman and two kids, even if I was her daughter. My lack of independence caused me to drown in a deep depression. I drank bottles of wine like it was a glass of water. I chained smoked cigarettes, and I pretty much fell apart. I may have seemed to have it together in the eyes of others, but that was far from the truth.

My mother worked nights, so most nights, we had the place to ourselves. There was a sadness I saw in my eyes every time I looked in the mirror. The look always crushed me, and it was like looking at a stranger. I would squint my eyes and smile at myself to remove the sadness, but it was still there. I felt lost and confused. I couldn't understand how I could have so much ambition and strength, but I felt like I was going backward. I found myself venting to the Moscato bottle. I worked in Annapolis, which was a 45-minute ride on a good day. The job paid decent money, but the travel time was beyond annoying. I didn't complain, and it felt good to have a job after many months of searching.

My mother lived across the street from my Aunt Shelby's old house, where I used to live. I didn't particularly care for South Baltimore. The people were trashy, and the way they did things were foreign to me. It reminded me of when I was young, and I got jumped at the school by a group of envious chicks for no reason at all. I didn't want my son to go to that same school. I kept him in Collington Square elementary over East Baltimore. The school over East had more of the community involved, although it was still in the hood. The decision to keep Zi in kindergarten on the other side of town was a headache and a huge inconvenience. Luckily, my mother took him to school for me after she got off the night shift.

It was a beautiful summer day when I decided to walk to Westside Shopping center. I didn't feel like driving. I wanted to walk through the hood and get some fresh air. I had swallowed two bottles of Moscato like there was no tomorrow, and the wine made me hungry. I figured I would walk to the Chinese joint and order some shrimp and broccoli with white rice. Whenever the weather breaks in Baltimore, people come outside like a gang of roaches. The amount of noise could be alarming for a visitor. Guys were yelling, "Blue Tops!" which stood for pills of dope. Random people were walking in the street, completely avoiding the traffic light. Girls were cursing out their kids or starting fights with random people who walked by. Dope fiends leaned over so far to the ground; it's almost unreal how they were able to keep their balance. It always amazed me to watch them lean without falling; instead of laughing at them, I acknowledged that humans are powerful. If they were sober, they could never keep such a balance. The cars rode by with the music blasting and random people screaming random remarks from the window. The chaos I witnessed while taking this stroll was the usual neighborhood behavior, so I bopped by like nothing was happening around me. I made it to the Chinese joint, which was crowded and extremely hot. There was no air, and the door was closed, which instantly felt like suffocation.

"Open up this mother fucking door. Shit, it's hot in here. Y'all love taking our money but can't even put a fan in this Bitch for your customers!" A young guy yelled out in the Chinese joint.

"Hell yeah! They know black people draw out the heat," an older guy with holes in his pants and a dingy white oversized shirt agreed.

"Man, they are taking forever. What the fuck! Shorty did you order?" the young guy aggressively asked, looking at me.

"No, not yet. I'm waiting for them to come back to the front," I responded.

"Mama! What the fuck, come on! It's hot out here. Do you see all of us waiting?" the young guy rudely asked. The woman spoke loudly in her language and took her time coming to the front as the young guy continued to complain.

"Excuse me, don't I know you?" a mild voice asked me while tapping my shoulder.

"Oh, my God. Hey Nikki! How are you, Girl?" I asked with excitement.

"Girl, I'm good. I haven't seen you in forever," Nikki replied.

"I know it's been years. Do you have any kids? How is your mother?" I asked Nikki while glancing at the rude guy who was getting louder by the minute.

"My mother is good, and you know her butt is still crazy. I have four kids, all girls. What about you?" Nikki asked as she looked at the menu.

"I have two. A boy and a girl," I replied as I looked at my phone to see the time.

"Guess who asks about you every time I see him?"

"Who?" I asked with a puzzled look.

"You know who. Chico, that's who," Nikki replied with a smirk.

"Oh, My Chico. I used to love that boy. You still be seeing him? You still hang up, Irvington?"

"Yup, I have an apartment up there. You know Chico always loved you. Please let me give him your number for the next time I see him."

"Hell yeah, you can give him my number. Put it in your phone. That was my heart back in the day. Do you remember when we met, we were up the Village at that party? I drove you crazy all night talking about him."

"How could I forget? Y'all both were annoying as hell. Starring at each other like some damn fools," Nikki said with laughter.

"I know, right. That was puppy love. What's up with him now? Do he have any kids?"

"I see you didn't change. You still have a hundred questions. You not going to pluck my nerves while we wait in this hot ass store," Nikki said in a sarcastic tone.

"You funny and still too damn smart. For real, does Chico have any kids? I'm simply curious," I asked with a sneaky smirk.

"Yeah, he has five kids. He turned into a slut bucket!" Nikki Sarcastically answered.

"Yuck, that's okay! Don't give him my number. Act like you never bumped into me," I laughed as I walked up to place my order finally.

"You are still crazy. I'm just joking. I think he only has a son. He was getting this number anyway so he can stop bugging me every time I see him."

"You play too much. Thank God he doesn't have five kids. That's a headache I damn sure don't want."

Nikki and I continued to have small talk. We opened the front door; we stood in front of the store to continue our conversation as we waited for the food to get done. As soon as we opened the door, we realized it was a hot summer night, and the burst of the air we hoped for didn't exist. Instead, we felt a musky humid breeze that barely blew. We agreed to hang out now that I was back in the area.

I continued to go to work and save my money. My mother didn't want my money, but I made her take it. It felt good to help my mother with her bills. A few weeks had passed since I last saw Nikki. I sat on my mother's sofa, watching family feud when the phone rang. It was an unfamiliar number, so at first, I rejected it. The number called right back, so I decided to answer.

"Hello," I answered in an annoyed tone.

"Sunni?" the guy questioned.

"Yeah, this is Sunni. Who is this?" I asked straight to the point.

"This is Chico. What's up?" he said with excitement.

"Oh, what's up, Chico?" I asked as my heart dropped into my stomach. I turned the TV down and walked to the kitchen so that I could talk in private.

"Girl, I never stop thinking about you. I was so damn happy when Nikki gave me this number five minutes ago!"

"Five minutes ago? You weren't playing, huh?" I asked while laughing.

"Nope, not playing at all. How you been? When can I see you?" Chico asked impatiently.

"I 've been cool. I don't know," I shyly responded. My nerves were getting the best of me.

"Where you stay now?" he questioned.

"Shit has been a little crazy for me. I'm down my mother's house right now," I said in an embarrassed tone.

"Where does your mother live? I'm trying to see you tonight," Chico expressed with excitement.

"She down by Westside shopping center, but I'm about to make this run. I can't do tonight," I lied.

"Well, come see me before you go on your run. I live up here by Beechfield," he persistently asked.

"Who do you live with?" I quizzed.

"Just me and my brother Nick. Come on, just stop through for five minutes," Chico pleaded.

"Tonight, is no good. I have so much to do. How are Shawny and Tori doing? Is Shawny still crazy? I miss her."

"You know her ass still crazy. So, you really not going to come see me?"

"I see you still don't give up. Okay, I will stop through for five minutes, but come outside, so I can hurry up and make my run."

"I can't wait. I'm excited like a little kid," Chico replied.

"I do have one confession before I come. I gained a lot of weight, and I look totally different now," I lied to hear his reaction.

"I still want to see your big ass. I don't care about that. Hurry up," he laughed.

I drove to Chico's apartment. My heart was thumping, and my skin crawled with anxiety. Flashbacks of our childhood crossed my mind, and I smiled with excitement. I knew it was a possibility I wouldn't even like him anymore. I knew he couldn't possibly be the young guy I once was head over heels for, but I hoped for some type of chemistry. I was nervous, and my stomach fluttered with butterflies. I rode around the block to avoid going to his place. I thought of turning around and meeting up with him another day. I was an adult, and I was far from the shy type, but I couldn't shake my nerves. He called questioning where I was, so I stop avoiding his apartment building and drove up to the building and parked. Before I could call to say I was outside, he was coming out of the building, smiling.

I immediately sized him up. Chico's caramel skin reflected off the building lights. He was still slim, but he was much taller. He grew into his height; he wasn't a short boy anymore. He had golds in his mouth, and his smile was still warm and comforting. His braids were gone, but he had a nice fresh haircut that flattered his face structure. He opened the passenger door, and I smiled. He instantly hugged me, and instead of me letting go, I held him tight. He didn't resist the embrace; instead, he held me back. We hugged for what felt like hours. He eventually let go and looked me up and down.

"I see you got jokes, huh? What weight you gained?" he laughed.

"You know I play a lot. You look the same, just more mature," I said with a smile.

"You look the exact same too. To be honest, you look much better," Chico said with a smirk.

"What are you trying to say? I wasn't cute back then?" I asked in a joking tone.

"Hell no. You were cute, but damn, you just look better," Chico smiled.

"Uhm, okay. I guess I would prefer to look better now. So, what's up? I'm a little nervous," I honestly stated.

"For real? You don't look nervous."

"Feel my hands. They are sweating!" I reached my hand out to Chico.

"Damn, they are sweaty. I'm a little nervous too. I'm so happy to see you," he smiled.

"Yo! Your hands are still soft like a baby's ass. You remember I would always say that?" I joked.

"Yup. I remember. So, when can I see you again?"

"I don't know. What's your situation? Are you with someone?" I nervously asked, afraid of the answer.

"No, I just broke up with my girl a few months ago, but it's complicated. I have a son, but that's about it."

"Complicated? How old is your son, and is he with your ex-girlfriend?"

"No, I don't have any kids with my ex. My son is almost three," he quickly answered.

"That's cool. I bet he is a cutie. Anyway, we have been talking for hours. I better get out of here. I never did make that run," I stated.

"Damn, I'm sorry. We got caught up going down memory lane. I wish I could kidnap you for real," Chico stated with a flirtatious face.

"I wish you could too. Oh, I have another confession! I didn't really have a run to make. I was just nervous."

"You are still very honest, I see. I have a confession too. I wasn't really sorry that you missed your run," he laughed.

Chico and I talked in the car for hours, and it was like we hadn't spent one day apart. His vibe was different, but his heart was just as pure as the day I met him. At one point, his lips were moving, but I didn't hear one word he said. I was indulging in his presence, his scent, his posture, and the way he smiled. I was scanning every inch of his existence. I silently watched his eyebrows move up and down with the expressions of his face. I admired his deep voice, which was still soft and humble. His complexion was just as milky as I remembered, but his lips were dark like he smoked a lot of weed. I imagined I would fuck him right there in the car. He said something that snapped me out of my fantasy. I smiled and nodded as if I heard him.

I ran into Chico one other time in the past when I was about 16 years old. I gave him my number, and he met me at my Aunt Shelby's house. I had been talking to grown men, and Chico seemed immature compared to the dope dealers I was dating. He seemed like he wouldn't understand the damage I had encountered over the years. Chico was still in puberty stages, his face was experiencing teenage pimples which I didn't care about, but it reminded me he was young. His conversation lacked maturity, and he talked like a teenager. I was working a job, and I talked like an adult. My childhood personality was pretty much gone. It wasn't anything wrong with him; he was acting his age. I was just overly mature. His lack of maturity turned me off, so we had no chemistry.

He caught the bus to come and see me that day. He wore an oversized shirt and rough looking jeans. The jeans almost looked like he had been painting or something. We sat in the basement and talked. The chemistry was off, the conversation was off, and the attraction was off. I assumed maybe all we had in the past was only puppy love. He was super affectionate and played with my fingers as he talked. The old me would've yearned for that type of touch from Chico, but I didn't like it, and I wanted to run. He stayed for a few hours before he started feeling my energy, and then he respectfully left. I walked him to the front door, and we kissed on the lips. Before the kiss, I just wanted him to go. After the kiss, I instantly felt butterflies, and it dawned on me that he was "My Chico." He turned to walk out the door, and I grabbed him back and hugged him tightly. I apologized for being a Bitch, and he said it was okay. We never talked again until this day.

The Chico I sat in the car with was not a little boy. He had matured into a grown man, and our attraction was instant. We both struggled to part ways, and we talked on the phone the entire night until I heard him snoring in my ear. We text all day while I was at work. This was the beginning of the Chico chronicles. There was one massive problem with our fast reconnection; he loved her too. I popped in his life with no warning. He already had deep feelings for the girl he had been dating for two years before Nikki decided to play cupid. She loved him too. How could she not? He was loveable. He downplayed whatever they had, and I accepted what he told me. No one existed in our private world but us. I can only speak of our connection.

We started talking on the phone all throughout the day, and it became normal to look for his calls or texts. Unlike a lot of guys, Chico liked talking on the phone instead of just texting. He wanted to hear the tone of my voice. I enjoyed his conversation, and he always made me laugh. He was still just as goofy as he was when we were younger, except now he had swag. I appreciated his not so serious attitude. A few weeks went by, and I decided to fake sick, and I left work early. I called Chico on my break before I put on my Oscar-worthy ill performance. He told me to play hooky at his house because he had called out of work too. I was nervous but agreed. We had been talking dirty about how we were going to do this and do that sexually, so I knew that day would be the day.

Here's where my mind went utterly nuts with anxiety and questions. *What if his dick didn't grow since we were 12? What if he can't fuck? What if he just wants to kiss the entire time? Oh, God, I hate extreme kissing. Shit, he's probably wack. Let me just call him back now, so I don't lose this feeling for him. Even if he is terrible in bed, I can teach him. Nope, I'm going anyway. Sex is not everything. No matter what happens, he's still My Chico.* My phone rung, which pulled me back to reality. It was Chico confirming that I was on my way. I couldn't understand why I was so nervous. I had two kids, and I was greatly confident in the bedroom. It's not like I was an inexperienced virgin.

I got to his apartment, and he welcomed me with a tight hug. He sat at the table, eating a bowl of "OOPS ALL BERRIES Cap'n Crunch," cereal. I sat across from him, watching him crunch and dip the spoon in the bowl repeatedly. He didn't say anything. He just looked at me and crunched.

"You want some?" Chico asked.

"No, I'm good. You are fucking that cereal up, though!" I laughed.

"This is my favorite cereal. I eat cereal every day. I love it!" he exclaimed.

"I see. It smells like a weed dispensary in here. You just finished smoking?"

"Yup. It's a half a blunt already rolled. You trying to smoke?" Chico asked, pointing to the ashtray.

"Sure. Do you have a lighter?" I questioned.

"Yeah, it's one in the room. Come on," Chico said as he threw the bowl and spoon in the sink.

"I see you still hate washing dishes," I smirked after looking at all the dishes piled up in the sink.

"Damn, you remember that?"

"Boy, I remember everything about you. I have what they call the gift of memory. It's sick how much I remember," I said as I followed Chico to his room.

"Well, I'm a leave you with a new memory for today," Chico expressed with flirtatious eyes.

I blushed and sat on his bed. We smoked, and I instantly felt regret. Certain grains of weed made me overthink or get paranoid. At first the high wasn't a good high. After we smoked, we talked for about 15 minutes before Chico got on the floor and pulled my pants down. I looked him in his eyes and said nothing. It was silence in the room, and I relaxed for the first time since being around him. He rubbed his hands up and down my thighs; then he kissed them. I squirmed around from the excitement of his soft lips.

"Be still," he softly said.

I listened like the sex servant I planned on being. Chico telling me what to do turned me on. I laid still as I felt the first kiss to my clitoris, it was soft and hot, and it was the best my girl had ever encountered. I tried to move away from the intense sensation my body felt from his pleasing mouth. I scooched my butt back to run from his daring tongue. The more I ran, the closer he grabbed me.

"Be still, I said," he calmly repeated.

I laid there in stillness. I released the tension in my body and let Chico take full control as he sucked my body into exhaustion. He stood up to walk away, but I grabbed him and let his boy indulge in my pleasing mouth. I sat on the end of the bed as he stood tall, enjoying the feeling of my secret weapon. Now he was the one pulling back, almost running from my tongue's sensations twirling around the head of his boy.

"Be still," I calmly whispered.

He smiled at me and fought the urge to squirm around. He stood in stillness as I enjoyed the beautiful skin of his grown man's penis that had grown quite a bit since we were kids. I moved up the bed and felt a sense of excitement knowing I was about to finally feel Chico inside me after oh so long of being curious. Instead of Chico entering my overly wet vagina, he continued with four-play, which blew my mind. When his boy finally met my girl for the first time, she hugged him like a long-lost friend, and she showed appreciation for the long wait by immediately releasing all over his penis, and the party continued.

We tried every position, every angle, and every type of sex move we could think of. We fucked as if we would never see each other again, and it was all love. I went to the bathroom to wash up. Chico came in behind me and rubbed his finger against my neck just like he used to. I smiled. I turned to face him to say how good the sex was, but he kissed me before I could speak. He lifted me up on the bathroom counter, and we went at it again. We washed up and talked for a few minutes before I left to get my daughter from the babysitter's house. The workday was over. I couldn't believe the sex was that good. I left Chico's apartment with a swollen vagina and an open heart.

All night I replayed our "hooking work" sex. He called me the next morning, and we talked on my ride to work. Now we were together every other day. That fast, we were hooked. He was like an addiction. I wanted to be around him all the time, but I enjoyed missing him. This period was also weird because, out of nowhere, I became timid. Something happened to me when I moved out of my rat-infested apartment and lost my independence. My bold, funny, big mouth personality was gone. Life had shut me up.

I became quiet, and I had never been quiet my entire life. If I was at Chico's apartment and it was a house full of people I barely talked. I lost myself. I didn't realize how I had changed until other people always bought it to my attention. I overheard one of my co-workers talking to a patient at the office where I worked, and the patient described me as the "slim, quiet one." I remember thinking who the hell is she talking about. One day I was at Chico's apartment with my kids. Shawny and Tori were there along with some of him and Nick's friends. They played cards, and I sat there smoking a cigarette and drinking Moscato when Shawny looked at me with a curious facial expression.

"Dag Sunni. You quiet as shit now," Shawny said with laughter.

"What? I'm not quiet," I said in a defensive tone.

"Shid. I haven't heard you say more than two words all night. Ain't she quiet as shit now, Tori?" Shawny asked her sister.

"You are quieter, Sunni," Tori agreed.

"For real? Do you think I'm quiet, Chico?" I asked Chico.

"No. You not quiet with me," Chico replied, uninterested in our conversation.

"Maybe not with him. But you're way different than the Sunni I remember. You were fun, and you never shut up. I loved to hear you talk cause you was funny," Shawny explained.

"I'm still fun girl. I don't know what you are talking about," I said, hunching my shoulders.

"Nope, you different. Ain't she Tori?" Shawny asked.

"Shit, Shawny. People change. She grew up! Come on, man, now you are talking too much!" Tori yelled.

"Y'all still crazy," I laughed as I took another sip of the Moscato wine.

I sat at the table and thought to myself, *Shawny is right! I lost my spunk. Maybe it was all the death, or perhaps it was the shock of the rats, but something took my personality away. Why had I let life take "My voice?" Why did I let my circumstances silence me? Why am I smoking all these damn cigarettes? Why don't I laugh anymore? What happened to me?* I replayed Shawny's words over and over again. I told myself to be my old self and have fun. Nothing worked. It was phony. My laughs were weak, and my smiles were faint. I felt nothing. My mother noticed I was off as well. She frequently asked me, was I okay? In my mind, I was okay.

I knew I was temporarily living with my mother, but besides that, things seemed to be okay. I had a job making decent money, I had a car again, my kids were healthy, I had Chico back in my life, and I had money in the bank. But I wasn't okay. I was severely depressed. I tried to mask the depression with whatever temporary happiness I could find. It never lasted. I was in constant agony. I was literally suffering from a broken heart. Every traumatizing event I encountered; I just threw it under the rug. "Fuck it. Can't change it, so fuck it," was my motto. Although I couldn't change the things that happened to me, I needed to deal with them. I thought Chico could be my relief. I could get lost with him, and everything could be okay. Chico would not be my savior; he would not heal the damaged little girl in me; he would eventually add fuel to the fire.

I fell hard and fast for Chico. I was comfortable around him, and I loved his energy. He made me feel good, and his soft hands touching me could instantly change my day. He called me one day and told me he lost his job. He started getting down, and I noticed he too had a sadness inside of him. We had long intimate talks about everything. He once told how he loved weed more than food. Marijuana was his downfall, and he would spend his last dollar for the high. Chico and Nick had fallen behind on their bills, and with him losing his job, the pressure was on. He ran to the streets to improvise his income. That decision would later backfire. One weekend we sat on his couch bored as I watched him play a game on the PlayStation.

"Do you feel like going out?" Chico asked never looking up.

"Yeah. The kids are with my mother. We can go out for a few hours."

"Did you ever pop a Molly?" Chico asked still hitting the controllers.

"Nope, but I took an E pill before," I admitted.

"Did you like how it made you feel?" Chico quizzed with raised eyebrows.

"I loved it. That was years ago, though. Why?" I asked with a confused face.

"My homeboy gave me a Molly. I thought we could do one together and fuck like crazy when we get back," he laughed.

"I will take a piece. I never take a whole of anything. I never took a whole E Pill to this day; shit I don't even smoke a whole blunt. You see me putting the blunts out in the ashtray all the time," I joked.

"Yup. Soon as you put the blunts in the ashtray, I smoke them," he laughed as he threw the controller on the couch.

"Yeah, you need to stop doing that too. I be looking for my little roaches, and they be gone. So, let me see the Molly."

"Here it goes. It looks funny, right?" Chico handed me the hard Molly.

"Hell yeah, it looks like a stone. How the hell do we pop this?" I asked with a confused expression.

"Let is dissolve on your tongue," he said as he bit the stone and popped it on his tongue. He handed me the remainder.

"Yuck, it's nasty as shit! I'm about to just swallow it," I said with my face frowned up.

"No, don't just swallow it! You can deal with the taste. I need you to be where I'm at. We in this together."

"Oh shit, Chico! I see little elephants running around. Oh, fuck! Something is wrong." I yelled.

"Girl, stop playing. It doesn't work that fast," he laughed.

About 15 minutes later, we were in a twilight zone. My lips felt weird, and we regularly touched each other. Every touch felt intensified. Chico rubbed my ass, and it felt like an intense sensation shot straight to my clitoris. The high was amazing. We intended to drive to my mother's house so I could get dressed, but instead, we stood in the living room slow dancing to rap music. I had my head in his chest, and we were floating. I finally reminded him that we were going out. We changed the plans to just meet his friends at another spot where they could shoot pool.

We were out of our mind high. Everything moved slow and weirdly enough; we felt more connected. We arrived at the lounge and stayed in the parking lot, kissing for what felt like hours. We held hands while walking in. I watched him play pool while I drank a mixed drink from the bar. I watched his every move and admired his energy. I loved the fuck out of Chico, and my emotions were open for the world to see. I couldn't hide my feelings for him, and it drove me crazy. I knew he loved me too. We would argue about who loved who more. I would always tell him, "I love you like a fat kid loves cake." His response every time was, "I love you like Whitney loved crack."

We floated throughout the night off the Molly's, and we had passionate sex as the night slowed down. We did Molly's two more times on separate occasions, then we stopped. Chico and Nick eventually lost control of the bills at their apartment, and they moved out. Here's where things shifted tremendously. He came to stay with me at my mother's apartment for a few weeks. We knew the arrangement would never work, but I was moving out in a few weeks anyway, so we just tried to push through until I moved. We stayed at my father's house a few nights as well, so we could give my mother's house a break.

My mother worked at night, which was fine during the night; however, it was awkward for her to be home with Chico during the day while I was at work. Chico was looking for a job, and his lack of income started wearing down on him. He started going to the street to get money. I wasn't naïve, and I knew what was happening, and I talked to him many times about staying on the legal path. I wanted him to feel open to tell me anything, and sometimes nagging can break good communication. So, I chose not to nag, but I should've. I just voiced my opinion about going down the wrong road and encouraged him to keep looking for a job.

He called me one day and told me to come to the gas station in Edmondson Village so he could fill the car up with gas. He had a bank card, and the card initially declined. He tried again, and it declined again for invalid zip code. Finally, the card went through. I questioned who card he had, and he informed me he took it from a guy earlier that day. He said it didn't feel right and he felt bad for taking it. He also admitted he felt excitement and a crazy thrill from the power of the transaction. It was a short period of bad decisions. It was only about a month of "taking," which eventually caused two weeks of searching.

On this weird day, Chico's vibe was off. He said things had spiraled out of control, and he needed to stop everything. We sat in the car as he vented and broke down all the details of how things went too far in his life. He said he would never take anything from anyone again. He was done. I was happy and relieved. Chico laid low at my father's house for a few days before we returned to my mother's place. I went to work the next day, and he ignored my calls for the entire day. I started to worry, so I called his brother Nick who told me some bullshit about Chico sleeping all day.

I decided I wasn't going to play games with him, so I ignored his calls for the next few days. I was in my feelings, and I couldn't control how loving him drove me crazy. My mind was so foggy. It was hard to see clearly while being sucked up in Chico's world. He would sometimes call me 20 times in a row, and it broke my heart to see his face pop up on my cell phone and ignore it. I just wanted honesty, but did I really? I don't know if I could have handled his truth. We enjoyed our time together, and when he wasn't with me, that wasn't my job to monitor his every move. I was too gone to leave him alone, and he refused to let me go. We fed off each other's energy. The chase was everything for us. If I pulled away, he wanted me more, and the same applied to me.

These little fights caused temporary distance between us, which weirdly enough bought us closer together. The make-up period was terrific, and when we were around each other, it was like nothing ever happened. I couldn't stay upset with Chico when I was in his presence. It was almost impossible to hold a grudge. The moment I laid eyes on him, all was forgiven. I often wondered, was I more in love with the younger Chico, which would explain why I was so weak for the older Chico. I couldn't understand the magnet attraction I had for him.

I went over East Baltimore to have some fun and to get my mind off of Chico. It was a beautiful spring day, and I was having fun in Licia's house. I sat in her living room, talking trash, and catching up. Licia went to the bathroom, and someone knocked on the door. I got up to answer the door. I looked out the peephole and was surprised to see who was on the other side of the door.

"What's up Sunni! I haven't seen you in a while," Nico smiled.

"Hey, Nico," I dryly responded. I hadn't seen Nico in years, and we didn't stop talking on the best of terms.

"Why you say it like that? Where is Licia?" he asked, still smiling unbothered by my attitude.

"You know I don't fuck with you, Nico!" I bluntly said as I looked him up and down secretly admiring his dope swag and handsome face.

"I know you not still mad. That was years ago. You should give me some of that pussy. You know how we do!" Nico flirted.

"You funny. That'll be the day," I sarcastically replied.

Licia joined us and greeted Nico. They talked, and I eventually loosened up and joined in on their conversation. He spoke with Licia's kid's father, who was his cousin. I would randomly glance over at him, and we would briefly catch eye contact. It was something about Nico that always got to me. It was a weird attraction and an intense feeling I couldn't explain. I loved his realness, but I was still a little bitter at how I felt he played me by denying our slip up years prior. Over the years, I would run into Nico at Licia's house, and I was always happy to see him, but I would never show it. My chemistry with Nico reminded me of an old tree, the branches were bare, then the leaves slowly grew green and full, then they changed to bright colors, then they got crispy and died, then that season is over but another season is always soon to come.

I left Licia's house, and I finally answered Chico's calls. He said he missed me, and he wanted to get some of his things from my mother's house. He came to get some clothes from the basement. He was extra friendly and apologetic for disappearing. He said he was just stressed and overwhelmed. He told me he got a job at the supermarket, stocking the market on the graveyard shift. I was excited for him to get back on his feet. I was still upset with him, and I couldn't pretend everything was okay. He left with two black trash bags full of clothes. I cried soon as the door shut. I missed him like crazy and being mean to him was hurting me more than him. He told me he was staying up one of his home boy's houses near Reisterstown Road. I had a strong feeling he was lying. I didn't question him because I had every intention to cut him off. I didn't talk to him for an entire week. It almost killed me to ignore his calls, but I managed to keep my distance until...

CHAPTER 11

A FIRE MUST BURN

When you open your eyes bright early in the morning, and your mind instantly starts to race, you have no idea what mysterious event is coming for your day. You have no idea how unpredictable life can be. Every moment of this day will forever have a special part in my brain that will never be forgotten. It's the day I stopped ignoring Chico. I missed him to the point of no return and fighting the urge to resist him had become more than my heart could tolerate.

It was a beautiful spring day, and I was sitting on the concrete steps at my mother's house. I started taking my daughter's hair out so I could braid it up for the week. She sat in between my legs moving around like she had ants in her pants. My cell phone rang, and I saw Chico's face pop up on the screen. My daughter's face lit up as she truly adored Chico. She answered without hesitation and started talking his head off. Tira eventually handed me the phone.

"Hey, Chico, what's up?" I asked in a pleasant tone.

"Damn, I miss you. I'm so happy to hear your voice," Chico stated with excitement.

"I can't lie, I miss you too," I said in a low tone.

"For real? I thought you cut me off for good!" he protested.

"You know I'm weak for your punk ass," I said with laughter.

"Look, can we start over? I just miss you," Chico asked in a convincing tone.

"Chico, we can't start over without honesty. Where are you really staying?" I bluntly asked.

"I was uncomfortable staying at your mother's. I wasn't working, and it didn't feel right," he said with a sigh.

"I understand that. You still didn't answer the question."

"Meet me up, Irvington, and we can talk about everything. Please meet me," he pleaded.

"Okay, I'll leave out in ten minutes," I said as I grabbed all the hair stuff off the front steps.

"I love you. I'll be waiting at the liquor store."

"Love you too, Chico."

I took the kids in the house with my mother and told her I would be right back after I finished meeting Chico. My mother was happy I was meeting up with Chico. She knew how sad I was without him, and she thought I was too hard on him. I pulled up to the liquor store, and Chico stood there with a bright yellow shirt and a pair of light-colored jeans. He walked to the car smiling from ear to ear. Soon as he got in the car, he reached to kiss me. I moved my face back. He reached again, and I turned my face again. Instead, I wrapped my arms around him, and I held him tight, I smelled his neck which smelled like his usual scent of sandalwood oil. A man walked by the car and yelled, "Get a room!" We stop hugging and laughed at the funny man. Chico offered to buy me a bottle of wine before we left the liquor store, and I gladly accepted. He was so excited about going to work that night. For some reason, Chico was extra happy, and his spirits were high. It was more than just seeing me; he seemed to be in a perfect place mentally.

"Dag, you wouldn't even let me kiss you," Chico said while looking out the side mirror.

"I don't know where your lips been. You still haven't told me anything." I honestly stated.

216

"We will talk, and I'll tell you everything. I got these food stamps. You want a cold cut sandwich?" Chico asked.

"Look at you showing off. I get wine and a sandwich, now?" I joked.

We crossed the street from the liquor store and ordered two cold cut sandwiches from the corner store. We waited on the side, and Chico put his arm around my neck. His arm felt light as if he avoided putting all his weight on me. I felt him looking at me, and I avoided his eye contact as much as possible. I wasn't upset with him, but I didn't want him to think he could just disappear, and everything would be okay. Finally, I looked at him, and instead of saying something, I licked his cheek and laughed to break the ice.

"Why are you so crazy?" Chico laughed as he wiped his cheek.

"You weren't expecting that, huh? Why you keep looking at me like that?" I asked.

"I just missed you, that's all. I don't like it when you mad at me," Chico confessed.

"I missed you too. So, what are you about to do now?" I asked.

"I wanted to chill with you until my shift starts tonight. Can you drop me off at the job before 10:00?"

"Yeah, I can drop you off later. It feels amazing out here today. I have to finish taking Tira's hair out."

"I don't care. I can help you take her hair out. I miss her too!" Chico smiled.

We got our food and rode back to my mother's house. I grabbed a comb and a spray bottle and continued taking out Tira's hair. Chico sat next to me. He kept agitating Tira by touching her ears and tickling her neck. Tira laughed and fussed with Chico. They were close, and Chico cared for Tira. I cared for Little Chico as well. Both of our kids were three years old, and they got along well. Sometimes Little Chico didn't want to share Chico with Tira, but he always got over it. Zi looked at Little Chico like a little brother. I appreciated the love Chico had for my kids, and I equally loved his son.

Chico and I talked about everyday life stuff as I continued to do Tira's hair. He avoided the conversation of where he had been for the last week. I wanted to wait to question him after I finished Tira's hair, so she couldn't listen to our adult talk. He told me how he couldn't wait to go to work that night. He said it felt good to be back working, and the night shift was a breeze. He said he and his co-workers smoked weed on their 15-minute breaks, and he loved the fun environment.

"Should I take this $10 and ride up the way and get a bag to smoke later?" Chico asked with slight hesitation.

"Is that your last $10?" I asked.

"Yup! Do you feel like taking me up there?" he questioned with a grin on his face.

"You should just save that money for tomorrow. Smoke with your co-workers for free. You just started working."

"Yeah, you right! But I'll either spend the $10 now or tomorrow, so it doesn't really matter."

"So, why you ask me? You already had your mind made up," I asked with a smirk.

"Fuck it. I don't need the weed right now. I have enough to smoke before my shift starts, plus I want to chill with you for real."

"Exactly. Can you put those sandwiches in the fridge?" I asked. I had forgotten entirely about the food.

"Dag, I forgot about the sandwiches. I think I'm going to get the weed now. Can you ride me up there, please?" Chico asked with a puppy face.

"Damn, you quickly changed your mind. I need to finish taking Tira's hair out. You can take the car," I suggested.

"Okay, thanks. I'll be back in 20 minutes," Chico said as he kissed my cheek.

It was around 7:00 PM when Chico left. He didn't come back in 20 minutes that wasn't strange because it was a nice day outside and I figured he ran into his boys. I called his phone around 7:30 PM, and he said he was on his way. He came back around 7:45 PM and sat on the futon bed in my mother's living room.

"What's wrong? Did you get the weed?" I asked.

"Yeah, I got it. Look at these fat bags?" Chico said as he handed me a red bag stuffed with weed.

"Why you look off? Your vibe changed from when you left out," I questioned.

"I'm just tired. I just need to sit here for a minute," Chico said in a strange tone.

"You tired? Who was outside?" I quizzed with a curious facial expression.

"Everybody for real. I have my homeboy in the car, and he's going to pay me to hack him over West. I told him I had to ask you first. I'll put the gas in your car," Chico explained in a nervous tone.

"You have someone in the car, and you are just sitting here chilling? What homeboy? I don't need no gas," I immediately responded.

"Just a homeboy. I already bought him down here. Can I just drop him off? I'll be right back, plus me and you still need to talk."

"You can go ahead and drop him off. You have to be at work by 10:00, right?" I reminded him.

"Yup, I'll be back way before then. Shit, we need to make up too! You know what I'm talking about,"

Chico said as he slapped my butt before running down my mother's basement steps.

"What did you get from the basement? If we are making up, then you need to hurry up back," I eagerly stated.

"I didn't get anything from the basement. I put something down there with my stuff. Can I have a kiss before I leave? I wanted to kiss you all day."

I walked up to Chico and kissed him. He put his hands around my waist and held me tight. The hug felt different. Not too tight or not too loose, just different. He squeezed my butt cheeks, told me he loved me, and walked out the door. I smiled when he left. I thought to myself, *I love that crazy boy.* He left around 8:10 PM. Chico sent a text about 20 minutes after he left, it simply said, "I love you, and I'm so happy you let me see you today. Be back soon."

Around 9:00 PM, I started calling Chico's phone to see if he was on his way back. He didn't answer. I felt weird, and in the pit of my gut, something didn't feel right. I washed Tira's hair and decided not to worry. I picked my phone up after shampooing her hair, and I didn't have a missed call from Chico, so I called him again. Still no answer. So, I repeatedly called. Around 9:30 PM, someone answered but didn't speak. I heard a commotion and heavy breathing. I yelled in the phone with irritation, "Hello!" No response, just a dial tone from the person hanging up. I called back, and the phone's power was turned off, and I was being sent straight to voicemail. I panicked.

Chico had to be to work in 30 minutes. My immediate thoughts were, *I know he didn't take my car to go see a Bitch. He really must have lost his mind.* I called Chico's cousin Shawny who voice cracked as if she was sleep.

"Hey, Shawny. Sorry to be calling you, but Chico has my car, and he should've been back. He has to be to work in 15 minutes. He's not answering his phone, but someone picked up and hung up. I don't care who's he with at this point. I'm just worried, and I want him to bring my car back so I can go to work in the morning."

"Calm down, Sunni. Damn, you are talking fast. You said he's not answering his phone? Let me call him, and I will call Nick to see if he knows where he is," Shawny calmly responded.

We hung up, and I continued to call Chico's phone. I paced back and forth as I waited for Shawny's returned call. Now it was 10:00 PM and No Chico. I knew he would never miss work. I called my mother's job for the first time ever since she worked there. She came to the phone in a panicked voice.

"Sunni, what' wrong? Are the kids okay?" my mother immediately asked.

"Yes. Something is wrong! I feel it in my gut. Chico took my car to drop off his homeboy, and he never came back. He supposed to be at work right now!" I cried.

"Sunni, calm down. What time is he supposed to be at work?" she asked.

"10:00, and I can't calm down! Oh my God, where is he?" I cried.

"It's only 10:30, and his phone could've died, the car could have a flat. You don't know what happened, just stop crying," my mother said in a calming but frantic voice.

"But he left around eight something. Something is wrong! Chico, please call. Shit!" I said in a frustrating tone.

"Try to calm down, Baby…"

"Wait, Mommy, that's Shawny on the other line. I have to take this, call me back on your next break."

"Hello. Did you hear from Chico?" I asked Shawny soon as I answered the phone.

"No. Everyone said they saw him earlier, but that was it. He's not answering the phone for us either," Shawny replied

"Yeah, he went to get some weed earlier. Oh my God, Shawny. Something just doesn't feel right," I confessed.

"Calm down, Sunni, you are freaking me out now. I'm a give aunt Pear your number. Call me back in an hour if you don't hear from him.

I sat on the edge of my mother's bed smoking cigarette after cigarette. I watched the ashes burn down to the green line on the Newport 100. I was in a daze, and nothing made sense. I replayed our entire day up until the point he walked out the door, and it dawned on me that he said he was with a homeboy. I regretted not walking to the car to see who this homeboy was, but it wouldn't have changed the fact Chico was not back. It was around 11:50 when I received a call from Chico's mother, Ms. Pear. She questioned me like the FBI themselves. I would expect nothing less from a caring mother. I patiently told her our entire day together up until he walked out the door. I talked to his brother Nick and Shawny's sister Tori, and no one had heard from him.

On this beautiful spring day in the month of April, My Chico went missing. The torture began. Missing is not to be confused with the feelings of death. When someone goes missing, the grief process is horrific, to say the least. You have hope, you have ideas, you have mysteries, you have conclusions, you have theories, you have faith, but what you don't have is the person who is missing. Where was Chico? What happened on that beautiful day?

I didn't get any sleep; I stayed up crying and worrying. I called the police around 4:00 that morning, and they informed me he was not considered to be missing. He wasn't a child, or he wasn't mentally disabled, so he had the right to be wherever he was. I explained how it was out of his character, and they didn't care. They even said, "Ms. Connor, did you consider maybe he's with another woman? Maybe he doesn't want to be found." It took everything inside of me not to smack the cop for being so insensitive. I then called out of work. After two hours of sleep, I woke up to the reality that Chico had not returned. I prayed somehow it was just a nightmare, but it wasn't.

The word got out quickly that Chico was missing, and everyone's main priority was to find him. All his exes, including me, put our feelings aside and came together. We all wanted him to be found. We talked throughout the day, trying to come up with a game plan to find him. My mind was filled with clutter and confusion. I felt like I was in another world, and I could barely function. I hadn't taken a bath in 2 days, and I was barely sleeping. I went to Wal-Mart with my hair all over my head, a raggedy t-shirt, and a pair of jeans. I went to print out "Missing Flyers." I had issues with the machine not working, and it sent me over the edge. I slowly slid to the floor next to the copier, and I mildly screamed in the middle of the store. A girl walked up to me and grabbed my arm.

"Whatever it is, Sweetheart, it will be okay. Come on, get up," the girl said in a soft humbled voice.

"No, it won't! It will never be okay! What if he is somewhere laying in a ditch waiting for help?" I screamed as if she knew what I was talking about.

"God pulled me through some rough times, and it will be okay," the girl said in a lowered tone.

"He's waiting for me to find him. I know he is. Thanks for helping me up, but I'm not in the mood for the "GOD STUFF," right now!" I said as I wiped my tears and pulled myself back up to the copier.

"Okay, I understand. Just always know God is there," she stated as she walked away.

I started back trying to use the copier, and I softly cried. Another girl walked up and helped me print the "Missing Flyers." I quietly watched the papers come out of the machine with Chico's precious face on the thin piece of paper. I felt sick. I sat back on the floor in front of the copier as his flyers continued to shoot out. I felt so numb, and I can't even recall how I made it back to the rented van. Everything was a blur. I sat in the parking lot and cried for two hours.

I finally got the strength to drive off, and I went to meet up with Shawny, who was also a disaster. We started slowly passing out the flyers. We drove around every neighborhood in his area knocking on doors, hanging them in stores, and putting them wherever they would allow us to put them. I drove down the street and hit the breaks to avoid something in the road, and that's when it hit me. The flyers fell everywhere, and it was Chico's picture all over the car. I jumped out of the car and had the most significant breakdown. I started screaming and swinging. Shawny got out of the car and grabbed me.

"Why is his face on these fucking flyers? Why is he missing? Why is this happening?" I cried with slobber and tears.

"I don't know, Sunni. We have to stay strong. We must find him. He is waiting for us," Shawny softly cried.

"Fuck, Fuck, Fuck! I can't handle this shit. I'm falling apart. I'm not strong enough, Shawny. I can't do this. Oh my God, I love him. I love him so much. I just want to hug him. I can't believe this," I continued to cry.

"Come on, Sunni. Let's get out of the street. I know you love him. He loves you too. We will find him, I promise. We are done with the flyers for today. That's enough. Let's meet up with Nick and Tori," Shawny said as she hugged me in the middle of the street.

"I love you too, Shawny. I'm just so lost. Okay, let's go," I said in a weak crackling voice.

"Yup, you are still good and crazy. You were punching the shit out of those flyers. You ugly as shit when you cry too! Got damn!" Shawny joked to change the mood. We both burst out laughing.

"I needed that laugh. I do have the ugliest crying face," I snickered as I wiped my tears and sniffed the snot back in my nose.

We met up with Nick, Tori and some of Chico's other family and friends at the police station. They finally took us seriously and started a Missing Person's Case on Chico and my car. Nick and Chico were close like twins. They looked a lot alike, and they were close in age. Nick was having a hard time coping as we searched for Chico, but he was stronger than any of us. He had to be. He couldn't fall apart like everyone else, and we needed his strength more than he knew.

We did a massive search for Chico, and hundreds of people came out to look for him. We looked everywhere in the city where we thought a body would be. I had a lot of hope we wouldn't find a body because I knew in my mind Chico was alive. I played with the option of maybe he got kidnapped, ran off the road, and was in a ditch just waiting to be found; perhaps he was hurt in a hospital with no identity. The possibilities of where a person could be were endless. The search continued. The number of people who loved Chico was out of this world. It was like anyone he had ever met instantly loved him. The love was overwhelming. It was the one comforting feeling as the search continued.

Ten long, excruciating days had passed, and I was fired from my job. I hadn't been to work, but once since the day he went missing, and I fell apart so bad that they made me go home. The only thing I could think about morning, noon, and night was Chico. I opened the refrigerator, and I saw the two sandwiches Chico, and I had bought the day he went missing. We never got to eat them, and they sat in the same spot in the fridge where he left them. I couldn't remember the last time I had actually eaten. I barely ate, and I lost an absurd amount of weight in a fast amount of time. I was a stick overnight. I looked terrible, but I felt worse. I got questioned quite a bit from the police and Chico's family since I was technically the last person to see him before it was reported. Nick discovered who the homeboy was in the car with Chico, and he started working on his own investigation. My car was found with the keys dangling out the driver door but still no Chico.

Seven years ago, on this day in April, I had given birth to a beautiful little boy that allowed my heart to beat again. It was my son's birthday, and I somehow found the strength to order him a cake and try to celebrate his 7th birthday. I was on my way to pick up his cake, and I decided to try my best not to think of Chico. I only wanted to celebrate the life of my child. My cell phone rang as I pulled in the Giant Supermarket parking lot. It was the call I dreaded. It was the call I feared, it was the call I would have never wanted to answer, but it was the call I needed for closure. It was the call of DEATH! Chico was found dead after 13 days of being missing.

I sat in the parking lot and felt a broad range of emotions. I felt heartache, grief, relief, fear, closure, and pain. The pain was unbearable, and my heart felt cold. I was relieved he was found, but it caused great suffering to my soul. My mind immediately raced back to when we were young. I reminisced on the first day I met him at the house party in Edmondson Village when I was only 12 years old. How he stared me down, and how we danced to Usher song, "Nice and Slow." I thought about the times we wrestled and played. I remembered the day Los got killed, and we sat on the side of the building scared. I remembered all the spitty kisses we had and every goofy conversation we ever had. I remembered watching him play basketball at Beechfield rec or him laying in my lap while I played in his hair for hours. I remember the time we tried to lose our virginity but got caught by Tori. I daydreamed about his soft finger swiping across my neck always to let me know it was him. It was him! It was that little boy I loved from the very first day I saw his bright eyes; It was him. Then my mind raced to the adult Chico. The affectionate Chico. I thought of all the sex encounters we shared along with all the intimate moments. I laughed at us, popping a Molly, and cried at the thought of never talking to him again. I had a lot of memories to think of as I sat in the car filled with grief. I felt honored to have had such a piece of him in my mind. I was grateful to have known him, and I was sad to have lost him.

The entire community came together at Beechfield Elementary parking lot, and we mourned the loss of Chico. It was hundreds of people crowded around with heavy hearts filled with grief and emptiness. We all prayed he would be found safe, and we all dreaded any other conclusion. We felt disappointed about the end result. We leaned on each other for support during such a horrible time.

How Chico died, doesn't matter. What happened to him doesn't matter. Where he was found, doesn't matter. Who discovered his body, doesn't matter. He died, he left, he's gone. It was him. Chico's experience here on earth was over. A piece of me died on that day when My Chico died. I replayed that day in my mind a million times. I was glad I kissed him before he walked out the door because that would forever be my last kiss. Chico was found, but his death caused me to be lost. TAKING can cause looking, being found can cause getting lost, and a hot flame can cause a lot of heat; but a fire must burn, and the ashes will eventually blow away!

CHAPTER 12

A DAY I COULDN'T COME BACK FROM

It had been almost 7 years since Chico's death when I made the difficult choice to take someone's life. My eyes were puffy and sore from crying the night before. I stayed up all night, reflecting on my life, and I found myself in a puddle of tears. My eyes ached, and my face was swollen. I woke up troubled and distraught. I had a feeling in the pit of my stomach that this day would be different. I knew in my soul I would never be the same. Although I knew something was wrong, I went on with my day. I ignored the feeling and pulled my hair into a simple ponytail before leaving the house. I glanced in the mirror, and for the first time ever, I saw someone I never saw before.

I never thought I would commit murder, and I surely didn't anticipate the consequences of such an act. The crime wasn't premeditated, although some would believe it was. It was never even thought about before this day. I felt weird the entire morning as I tried to ignore the butterflies that so heavily laid in my gut. I was responsible for my actions, but I didn't want to be held accountable. I tried to blame life, my childhood, my environment, or even Baltimore. I couldn't blame anyone but myself. I am the one who grabbed the knife that slowly slit the throat of every horrific memory this person caused me. In my mind, I was protecting myself. It was life or death. It was her or me. I had to choose myself. I had my kids to think of. I had a family to live for. They would soon be disappointed because saving my life caused significant changes for theirs.

No one was prepared to build a relationship with a murderer. They tried to understand and sympathize with my decision. I saw a different look in their eyes, a look of fear, maybe even disappointment. My family and friends seemed confused. When all the smoke blew over, I thought they would have many questions, but they mostly said nothing. Their opinions wouldn't change anything anyway. I killed her. That can't be undone. No talking, questioning, or judging will undo what I did.

What everyone didn't know is this person was secretly hurting me. I took the beating over and over again until I couldn't. I never told anyone the pain she caused me, that was my fault. Maybe if I spoke up, there would've been less confusion. Perhaps she could've even survived, but I didn't speak up, and she's gone. I must live with her death, and so does everyone who loved her.

Some would say I fucked up. I would agree, I made a lot of mistakes. One of the most regrettable mistakes is taking her abuse for so long. I also didn't go over other options before I made the bold decision to end her chapter. Her story was over, her life was over, and she had no idea. She was just as blind and oblivious as everyone else. She thought I would let her keep hurting me. All I been through, she thought I would be that weak. No one knew I would lose my composure and snap. Maybe she would have treated me differently had she known on this day; I would snatch her breath directly from her lungs.

Maryland doesn't have a self-defense law, and I'm not surprised. This state is full of shit, and their laws are the biggest pile of crap I've ever smelled. I've been asked, "Why?" Some people don't know what I did. I honestly don't know if I was in the right frame of mind. I don't know what a typical frame of mind should think like. What haunted me is my lack of remorse. I remember that day so vividly in my mind, so here's how I got away with it.

The day I Killed Shai was a day I would never forget. I was sitting in the grass at Columbia Lake. The wind was slightly blowing, and the sun was shining directly on my face. I admired my surroundings. I sniffed the smell of the air, which smelled like trees and freshly cut grass. It smelled nothing like the harsh air in Baltimore that resembled Newport smoke and debris from gunshots. The calm vibes of the lake made me feel full of life. It was the day I realized I was alive, but she was dead. I realized I had killed her, and the fact I felt no grief was alarming. Maybe I should've been killed her. She died years ago when Row died, but I tried to save her. Everyone needed her to be who she was, so I kept her alive for everyone else. I kept her hidden so no one could know I was slowly killing her. No one would truly be ready to accept her death. The consequences of a murder would change my life and the lives of those who loved her. She had been molested, victimized, pitied, depressed, and broken.

Shai laid in pure agony and pain. She cried with a pathetic tone begging for survival. I prayed no one would hear her low cries. I prayed no one would come over and ask her, "What's wrong?" I wanted to silently kill her with no disruptions. Right before she took her last breath, her life flashed before her eyes. Her mind went back to the beginning when she had hope as a little girl that life would be great. She visualized sitting in the kitchen with her grandfather making sweet potato pie. She smiled at the thought of him taking his finger and wiping the pie off her cheek. She thought of Jazz and how she laid so lifeless in a coffin with a pink dress and chapped lips. She remembered what the evil devil did to her and how he tried to scorn her by stealing her innocence.

Shai lowered her head and smiled for the first time since her life had been threatened. She smiled at the fun she had with Honey growing up entirely too fast. She laughed at all the project fights and the house raids. She breathed heavily and lowered her head as she thought of Morris and their one and only kiss. She thought of the day her Uncle Tom gave up on life and how helpless she felt, which instantly gave her that uneasy feeling in her gut, the same uncomfortable feeling she got when she laid in the gutter after learning Row had his head blown off on the phone. Oh, how she loved Row, her first grown man. Her heart thumped with anxiety and fear as she thought of Marco and envisioned him taking his last breath of air while glaring in her eyes, which then bought her attention to her son. Thinking of Marco reminded her that her son would never have a father, and now he would be losing the only mother he's ever known. She found the courage to yell at me, her killer.

"I can still be great. Give me another chance! Please. I know how to get through life's pain. I promise," Shai begged with a frightful face.

"No, you can't. I tried to let you live. You are DAMAGED! This life is over for you."

Shai wept louder. She thought of her daughter and how young she was. It dawned on her that her daughter would only remember a piece of her. That scared her more. That thought carried her mind to the day she tried to commit suicide. She had promised to never be so weak again. Her stomach turned as she pictured the rat that laid lifeless on her kitchen floor. She remembered overcoming living next to a real-life stalker. She took a moment to reflect on how far she had come.

"I did a lot. I've accomplished a lot. I'm not all damage. I got through school; I moved my kids to a better environment. I have talents, I'm ambitious, I can still be great," Shai pleaded.

"I thank you for doing all those things. Your skills and ambitious mindset will never die. I promise to keep the good in you alive. I'm sorry, Shai, but I still must kill you."

"But why? Why am I not worth the fight?" Shai asked as tears filled her eyes.

"Life is too short, Shai. I wish you were able to deal with life as it came to you. You let it break you. You let it become you. You let death take over your life. Your time is up!" I softly whispered.

"Wait! Wait! Can I have two more minutes to reminisce before you kill me? Please. Just two more minutes," Shai begged as she tightly closed her eyes.

Shai closed her eyes before waiting for my response. She burst into laughter at the thought of her selling drugs. She laughed even harder at the days she tried to sell pussy. She smirked at her kinky wild ecstasy days. She felt proud of her stand up moments, like being the first student to finish high school at night or when she created change for her old job by recognizing Dr. Martin Luther King Jr. Those thoughts gave her a brief smile. Tears rolled down her cheeks as she thought of Chico, she remembered the first day she met him at a party and how handsome he stood with his bright eyes and beautiful brown skin. She remembered how he would rub her neck and hold her hand. Then she thought of the mature Chico, and she cried harder.

I smacked her out of her daydream because it was time for her to die, her death was coming, and her time was up. Enough reminiscing Bitch, you have to go. Fuck your story and your heartache. You may be wondering how did I kill her? How did I get away with it? I killed her by opening my laptop on the grass in Columbia at the lake, and I started typing my first novel titled "DAMAGED little girl." I never got professional therapy, and writing my story was my therapy, and it was also the death of my past, including who I use to be. Sadly, for Shai, she died right there with my history. The death of Shai was the birth of Sunni.

I never knew the freedom I would feel from releasing my old self. I became a dreamer. I never looked back. I changed my story, and I eagerly let go of the "Old story." I started my therapy by telling my story. It was harsh at times and pretty degrading. It was brutal and raw. In some chapters, I cried the entire section, but I kept typing. I knew the only way I could truly get rid of my old life was to face it. I held nothing back, and I let go of every embarrassing detail when I let go of Shai. I put my old life out there for the world to read and judge. I have no regrets; I only wish I could've killed the Bitch sooner.

Although I left my past behind, there was one tree that grew with me. Remember, I said Nico reminded me of a tree, well the seasons have changed again, and the leaves are beautiful. Nico held a piece of my soul all along, we weren't mature enough for our first season, but oh how the flowers bloom. We have blossomed into our season. Sometimes life already has a plan for you, and everything is unfolding beautifully. I am the happiest I have ever been my entire life. I am living my dreams, I am successful, I am loved, I am free, I am an author, I am a play writer, I am a motivational speaker, I am a producer, I am an amazing mother, I am an amazing daughter, and I am alive. They call Baltimore the crab city. I was the one crab in the barrel trying to get out. Well, I did make it out. Meet Sunni! I'm a badass, beautiful, black woman who overcame my circumstances. I am Sunni T. Connor, an UNDAMAGED Woman.

~ ACKNOWLEDGEMENTS ~

I want to thank all my family, and friends for the support over the years. I want to thank my beautiful kids for being so lovable and patient with my busy schedule. I /want to thank my parents for allowing me to dream and loving me unconditionally. I want to thank every soul I met and lost; may you all continue to rest in peace. Thanks to Barbara for your continued encouragement, rest well, I can feel your presence everywhere. Lastly, special thanks to BT, we are surely in the jungle Baby.

~ TO MY READERS ~

Thank you for reading my life story. I appreciate the time you invested in reading my books. Without your support, it would be impossible for me to succeed as an author. I humbly say thanks for all your support.

Want to read more?

Check out "*DAMAGED little girl*," the prequel to this book.

Look out for my next book titled "*Who The Fu*k Is Society.*" It's a self-help book which encourages you to be your best you. It also explains how I went from DAMAGED to a DREAMER!

Need some quick entertainment?

Check out these links

https://www.youtube.com/watch?v=wF9ti9Bj_yO&t=98s

Please come see my play, "DAMAGED," in a city near you!

Stay in Contact!

Visit www.naturallysunni.com or text Sunni to 59769 for more info.

IG @naturallysunni32
FB @Sunni Connor
damagedlittlegirlbook@gmail.com